THE EXECUTIVE'S GUIDE TO 21ST CENTURY CORPORATE CITIZENSHIP

How Your Company Can Win the Battle for Reputation and Impact

As long term investors, we at Trillium Asset Management believe that well managed companies understand both sustainability risks and opportunities. *The Executive's Guide to 21st Century Corporate Citizenship* is an essential resource for those seeking to learn how to manage these material issues and how to develop collaborative relationships with key stakeholders — including investors. At the end of the day it is this partnership that fosters the innovation necessary to make the transition to a truly sustainability economy.

— Paul Hilton, Portfolio Manager,
Trillium Asset Management

Dave Stangis and Katherine Smith bring together a powerful combination of leadership, knowledge and experience in the arena of building sustainable shared value through business. This book offers a terrific opportunity to take advantage of their years of experience and thus shortcut your path to becoming a more sustainable brand.

— KoAnn Vikoren Skrzyniarz,
Founder/CEO Sustainable Life Media

21st century investors are seeking sustainability leaders to realize stronger, more resilient portfolios that can deliver lower future risk and potentially higher financial returns. Stangis and Smith's *Executive Guide to 21st Century Corporate Citizenship* is an essential how-to guide for Boards, chief executives and managers to learn how to embed this leadership for shareholders and stakeholders, and for chief sustainability officers to build and implement comprehensive strategies for success in concert with people, planet and profit goals.

— *R. Paul Herman, Founder and CEO,*
HIP (Human Impact + Profit)
Investor Ratings and Portfolios

This book is important because it offers a step-by-step approach to thinking beyond the quarter to nurture the long-term health of the company, its suppliers, and its customers. It helps the corporate citizenship manager consider all the operation's dimensions, methodically assess the operating environment, and develop objectives and a plan to improve both the business and the world.

— *Denise Morrison, President and CEO,*
Campbell Soup Company

Because of the magnitude of the challenges and opportunities we face as a society corporate citizenship professionals must be excellent leaders and managers both. This book provides an excellent toolkit to support the important work of our next generation of corporate citizenship leaders — no matter which seats they occupy in their companies.

— *Andy Boynton, Dean,*
Carroll School of Management,
Boston College

THE EXECUTIVE'S GUIDE TO 21ST CENTURY CORPORATE CITIZENSHIP

How Your Company Can Win the Battle for Reputation and Impact

BY

DAVE STANGIS
KATHERINE VALVODA SMITH

United Kingdom — North America — Japan
India — Malaysia — China

Emerald Publishing Limited
Howard House, Wagon Lane, Bingley BD16 1WA, UK

First edition 2017

Reprints and permissions service
Contact: permissions@emeraldinsight.com

British Library Cataloguing in Publication Data
A catalogue record for this book is available from the British Library

ISBN: 978-1-78635-678-9 (Print)
ISBN: 978-1-78635-677-2 (Online)
ISBN: 978-1-78714-300-5 (Epub)

ISOQAR certified
Management System,
awarded to Emerald
for adherence to
Environmental
standard
ISO 14001:2004.

Certificate Number 1985
ISO 14001

INVESTOR IN PEOPLE

CONTENTS

SECTION 1

LAYING THE FOUNDATION AND GIVING YOUR TEAM THE RIGHT TOOLS

SECTION 2

GETTING RESULTS ACROSS YOUR BUSINESS

SECTION 3

PULLING IT ALL TOGETHER

FIGURES AND TABLES

FIGURES

TABLES

Chapter 4

FROM THE CORNER OFFICE

The Boston College Center for Corporate Citizenship is
fortunate to have a network of more than 430 member
companies that they can call upon for insight about effective practices. We are delighted to share insights that key
executives from selected member companies have shared
with our membership in recent years.

FOREWORD

From Denise Morrison
President and Chief Executive Officer
Campbell Soup Company

I am honored to contribute to the foreword of this book with Andy Boynton, Dean of Boston College's Carroll School of Management.

The Executive's Guide to 21st Century Corporate Citizenship — How Your Company Can Win the Battle for Reputation and Impact ties together important principles that have informed and guided my career.

As the CEO of Campbell Soup Company, I work with this book's coauthor, Dave Stangis, Campbell's Vice President of Corporate Responsibility and Chief Sustainability Officer, to set our corporate citizenship agenda. I am thrilled Campbell was able to attract Dave, one of the field's most respected professionals. He is passionately driven to make our company — and the world — better every day.

As a proud alumna of Boston College, I have also followed the admirable progress of the Center for Corporate Citizenship — run by Dave's coauthor Katherine Valvoda Smith. My time as a BC undergraduate reinforced the importance of doing right while doing well. Those ambitions and values led me to Campbell, a company that embraces the values of service leadership and promotes them through our Purpose — Real Food that

Matters for Life's Moments. Our Real Food philosophy embodies creating real food that is affordable and accessible for consumers, respecting the environment, and innovating to improve the quality of life and well-being of our customers and employees.

Our society stands at the intersection of global consumer demand, technology, environmental sustainability, and human well-being. With markets moving at the speed of ideas, it's difficult to predict where the next disruptive innovation or seismic shift will happen. It is an interesting environment for a nearly 150-year-old company with several of the world's most recognized and respected brands. For me, building on the Campbell legacy to develop our 21st century corporate citizenship strategy has reinforced the business and social good that can be realized when we live our Purpose, not only in the short term, but also for generations to come. I believe you can make a profit and make a difference.

This book is important because it offers an executive overview of how to organize to think beyond the quarter to nurture the long-term health of the company, its suppliers, and its customers. It helps the corporate executive consider the operation's dimensions, assess the operating environment, and develop objectives and a plan to improve both the business and the world.

At Campbell, while our business strategy may shift over time and across markets, our Purpose and commitments to corporate citizenship will continue. We are tremendously proud of our environmental sustainability, public policy, and community achievements, and we know that our leadership differentiates us with many stakeholders.

Will it be difficult? Of course. Will it require time and effort? Of course. But we'll never stop trying to improve. I encourage you, and all readers of this book, to join our efforts, leveraging this invaluable resource. It's the right thing to do for all of us — for our consumers, our companies, our shareholders, and our planet.

From Andy Boynton, PhD
John and Linda Powers Dean
Carroll School of Management
Boston College

As Dean of the Carroll School of Management, I am pleased to contribute this foreword alongside one of Boston College's must accomplished alumnae, Denise Morrison. Denise has made important points about the challenges we face and the value of this book in our business context.

The Executive's Guide to 21st Century Corporate Citizenship — How Your Company Can Win the Battle for Reputation and Impact is a unique resource for leaders who want to maximize business and social value and who see the opportunity to use the assets of business to solve some of our most pressing environmental, social, and policy problems.

Through the work of its Center for Corporate Citizenship, Boston College has been committed for more than 30 years to help companies make more effective social and environmental investments. We've been proud to have Dave as a longstanding member of the Center's Executive Forum and Katherine Valvoda Smith has done an excellent job as its executive director. Their collaboration offers a privileged perspective on the business of corporate citizenship. Dave has worked at the top of his field in three companies and in many industries. Katherine has had the opportunity to observe thousands of individuals across hundreds of companies and to interact directly with dozens of projects. Together they bring almost six decades of insight and experience to this book.

This is an important book for executives who find they want to or need to refresh their company's corporate citizenship strategy. Their companion book — *21st Century Corporate Citizenship: A Practical Guide to Creating Value for Society and Your Business* — offers a comprehensive process for your teams engaged in executing corporate citizenship programs. This book helps the executive guide the strategy to be executed.

Corporate citizenship has evolved quite a bit in the 30 plus years that the Center has been in existence. Even 10 years ago, I — and many other management professors — might have considered environmental, social, and policy considerations secondary to business strategy. Today, managing these domains is essential to business strategy. This book offers practical guidance to business leaders about how to consider these domains within your strategy.

At its heart, corporate citizenship is change management. It is about envisioning a different and better future for business and society. Change management requires the skills of both leaders and managers. Warren Bennis, one of the pioneers of contemporary leadership studies, was fond of saying, "The manager does things right; the leader does the right thing."

Bennis is right. We need not just to do things right —
which is about execution. We must do the right
things, which means finding better ways to carry out the
missions of our organizations. Without leadership, there's
no agenda for change and improvement. There's no
vision.

In my research, I've developed a list of three things any
leader must do to be more than a manager. These reflect
my three decades of working with leaders worldwide as a
speaker, author, strategy professor, executive trainer, and
dean of a management school.

Leaders Stake Out a Clear Vision
It's simply impossible for organizations to do great things
if they have no clear expectations of the future. Without
a vision, people lurch in different directions or run in cir-
cles. The result is a waste of time, money, and brain-
power. Visions focus minds, hearts, and energy.

Leaders Get the Architecture Right
They design organizations that create the space for talent
to soar. At a minimum, leaders remove all of the road-
blocks that people must work around to do their jobs.
The obstacles could be inadequate information, conflict-
ing goals, mixed signals from the top, or confusing
reporting relationships.

Leaders Call for Leadership from Every Seat
They make it clear that everyone should step up and
find their spots as leaders, regardless of rank, title, or
position. This is especially true when it comes to generating ideas.

Because of the magnitude of the challenges and opportunities we face as a society — overpopulation, climate change, inequality, water scarcity — successful executives must be both excellent leaders and managers. This book provides an excellent tool kit to support the important work of our next generation of corporate citizenship leaders — no matter which seats they occupy in their companies.

ACKNOWLEDGMENTS

We would like to thank many people and organizations who contributed to this book. Thanks to Mike Sugarman for suggesting the project and being a great optimist and enthusiast for the field and for the work of the Boston College Center for Corporate Citizenship. To our current bosses (Katherine, Carroll School of Management, Dean Andy Boynton and Dave, Campbell Soup Company President, and CEO Denise Morrison) for their belief in the importance of the project and their support. To our excellent first readers, Steve Quigley, Jessica Shearer, and Kate Rubin, who offered great feedbacks and ideas. To our Emerald Insights editors, John Stuart and Pete Baker, for their patience and advice. To Sara Henry and Liz Rogers for their contributions to the materiality chapter. To all of those who read drafts and offered ideas and insights: Dan Bross, Suzanne Fallender, Rick Pearl, Regina McNally, Marcia Ryan, James Valvoda. To all of our colleagues who assisted with the "From the Corner Office" entries.

From Dave to Carolina, Michael, Megan, and Dad for providing the inspiration for, and for instilling, the work ethic and value set to live by. From Katherine to Ted and Casey Smith for their patience, love, support, and forgiveness for the absentminded responses to questions, postponed family outings, and evenings at the computer rather than the family table.

To all of our former bosses, who allowed us to disrupt, challenge, persuade, and work above our paygrades (although clumsily at times) on the topics and issues outlined in this book. Your faith that we would actually make things a little better than how we found them helped us learn and grow as professionals.

INTRODUCTION

We have always had a strong belief that the science and art of corporate citizenship are fundamental to differentiated business success. This has played out in our personal careers and in the careers and companies we've had the opportunity to influence. As we started to talk about the need for a "how to" book that addresses the fundamentals of corporate citizenship practice, we realized that the two of us had, between us, almost 60 years of experience working in some dimension of corporate citizenship. Although Dave started in environmental health and safety management and Katherine in philanthropy, their career paths converged at the intersection of those disciplines and corporate citizenship strategy. As a team, we drafted this companion to our book *21st Century Corporate Citizenship: A Practical Guide to Creating Value for Society and Your Business.*

This book is designed to provide a quick-hitting, one stop shop for the executives charged with getting the most impact out of their companies. It is the go-to resource for those senior executives, CEOs, or board directors, seeking to get the best out of your corporate citizenship team. We hope you will use this book as a resource that can help you think through the 21st century competitive dynamics that create the most value for your company, your shareowners, and society.

Dave Stangis is Vice President of Corporate Responsibility and Chief Sustainability Officer for the Campbell Soup Company. Campbell's portfolio of products extends beyond soup to foods such as Pepperidge Farm breads and Goldfish crackers; Arnott's, Kjeldsens, and Royal Dansk biscuits; V8 beverages; Bolthouse Farms super-premium beverages, carrots, and dressings; Garden Fresh Gourmet salsa, hummus, dips and chips; Plum organic baby food; Swanson broths; Prego pasta sauces; and Pace Mexican sauce.

Dave created and now leads Campbell's corporate social responsibility (CSR) and sustainability strategies. As such, he oversees the company's execution of CSR and sustainability goals, policies, programs, engagement, and reporting, from responsible sourcing and sustainable agriculture to social impact metrics in the community. Since arriving at Campbell Soup, the company has been named as the Dow Jones Sustainability Indices, the 100 Best Corporate Citizens List, the 100 Most Sustainable Corporations, and as one of the World's Most Ethical Companies.

For more than 20 years, Dave has been leveraging corporate responsibility principles to generate business and brand value. Prior to joining Campbell, he created and led the Corporate Responsibility function at Intel. He led a global CSR network organization, a role that gave him insight into corporate citizenship across the world. He's also served on the boards of Net Impact, the Graham Sustainability Institute at the University of Michigan, the University of Detroit-Mercy College of Business, the United Way of Greater Philadelphia and Southern New Jersey, and Ethical Corporation Magazine. In 2008 and

2013, he was named one of the 100 Most Influential People in Business Ethics by *Ethisphere Magazine*. *Trust Across America* named him one of the Top 100 Thought Leaders in Trustworthy Business Behavior for four years running.

Dave earned his MBA from the University of Michigan, his Master of Science in Occupational and Environmental Health from Wayne State University in Detroit, and his undergraduate degree from the University of Detroit.

Katherine Valvoda Smith is Executive Director of the Boston College Center for Corporate Citizenship in the Carroll School of Management. She oversees all the Center's activities and strategic ventures and teaches "Managing Business in Society" in the Carroll School of Management MBA program. The purpose of the Center is to help corporate citizenship professionals know more, do more, and achieve more with their corporate citizenship investments by understanding the foundations of how companies create good in the world and add value to their businesses through their environmental, social, and governance investments.

The Center has conducted research about the practice of corporate citizenship for more than 30 years, developing the deep knowledge and insights that help corporate citizenship professionals manage and improve performance in the environmental, social, and governance dimensions of their companies. The BC Center for Corporate Citizenship supports more than 430 (and growing) members each year; as its executive director, Katherine has had the opportunity to work with dozens of companies and to observe closely the corporate citizenship practices of hundreds of companies and thousands of practitioners.

Before joining the BC Center as Executive Director, Katherine held various academic and administrative positions in higher education and in nonprofit organizations. Throughout her career, Katherine has worked to support several large-scale public–private partnerships and research projects. These include a series of corporate, foundation, and university research partnerships focused on multidisciplinary science initiatives, and on social issues, including education and health care. She has also served as an advisor for numerous Fortune 500 companies. She earned her BA from Cleveland State University and her master's degree from Rhode Island School of Design.

THE EXECUTIVE BRIEF

We spend a lot of time within our own spheres at Campbell and the Center for Corporate Citizenship building models and strategies that deliver results ranging from reputation management and operational efficiency to employee and community engagement. We also spend a lot of time providing advice and structured programs to our peers and other companies about how to leverage these disciplines for true business value. We wrote this book for executives and managers who are seeking perspective on their company's corporate citizenship programs. If you are looking for the "how to" book, please pick up the companion to this volume: *21st Century Corporate Citizenship: The Practical Guide to Creating Value for Society and Your Business*. This book is for the busy executive or manager who is looking for a quick guide that can inform the questions they should be asking themselves and their teams to ensure that they are getting the most out of their corporate citizenship program, for their company and for society.

This is a book about building a successful business in the 21st century. It's a book about leveraging all the tools, trends, and assets at the disposal of business to drive bottom-line results, value chain resiliency, productivity, innovation, long-term shareowner value, and benefit for the community and a better world for all of us.

We will use terms like sustainability, corporate responsibility, and social impact to help explain our concepts and translate some of our frameworks, but this is all about creating the most successful business possible in the 21st century competitive landscape.

THE CORPORATE CITIZENSHIP CHALLENGE

What is corporate citizenship? You may have heard it called by a variety of names — corporate social responsibility, corporate sustainability, corporate responsibility — but all terms boil down to the same thing: building a more ethical, resilient, sustainable and profitable company. In the 1970s and 1980s, Corporate Citizenship, CSR, CR, etc. were a kind of shorthand for talking about corporate philanthropy. As the practice has evolved, so has the purview of the practice. Today when we talk about corporate citizenship, we are talking about how companies exercise their rights, responsibilities, obligations, and privileges across a variety of economic, social, and environmental domains.

In 1970, Milton Friedman wrote an article in *The New York Times* magazine titled "The social responsibility of business is to increase its profits." Wildly influential, this article argued that if businesses contributed to charitable causes, they would betray their primary responsibility as businesses: profit-making. Friedman left little room for considering that any environmental, social, or governance (ESG) expenditures might help a company's profit margins. That was the reigning assumption at the time, but what if Friedman were wrong, or the assumptions on which he based his argument do not hold today? What if strategic corporate giving and other ESG activities were not noble wastes of money? What if, instead, they actively create value for the company and society? Since Friedman made his assertions in the 1970s, social scientists have been searching for hard evidence linking ESG performance to financial performance. They have found a great deal of it; numerous empirical studies have indicated that it never hurts to do the right thing and it may, in fact, pay to do the right thing:

- The 30 years of research examining the relationship between corporate social performance (CSP) and financial performance (CFP) over 52 studies suggested that CSP and CFP generally go hand in hand, and this effect holds true across a variety of industry and study contexts.[1]

- A 2015 paper suggests that analyst evaluations of companies with poor social performance are less likely to carry buy recommendations even if the stock appears to be underpriced based on evaluation of the fundamentals.[2]

- A meta-analysis[3] of 35 years of research, looking at 214 studies, concluded that CSP has a positive relationship with CFP especially if the company can improve its environmental impact and is a transparent and proactive reporter of its ESG performance. In fact, the study notes that companies may under-communicate about their good works and could derive more value from strategic communication.

- Two recent papers[4,5] tracked the market's reaction to CSR-related investor engagements with publicly traded target companies. One study looked at 2,152 engagements with 613 firms between 1999 and 2009 — a very large sample for a study of its kind — the engagements were designed to improve the target company's CSP. Researchers found that successful engagements correlated to share price increase by an average of 4.4% in a year. The second, similar study found share prices to increase by an average of 1.7% per year.

Although few studies operate on scales as grand as the above three papers, the empirical relationship between corporate ESG and financial performance is consistently documented in current scholarly literature. A 2013 study,[6] for instance, focused primarily on CSR ratings; it aimed to disentangle various measures of environmental performance into a simpler, cleaner metric. Researchers distilled these diverse measures into two principal drivers: the adoption of environmental management practices and reporting and environmental outcomes (the tangible environmental outputs a company creates). They then investigated the relationship of these drivers to financial performance. They found a significant relationship between environmental processes and financial performance, indicating that firms can create more value by implementing environmental practices. Nearly half a century after Friedman's provocative article, the tables have decisively turned. Researchers have, time and time again, demonstrated that strategic socially responsible behavior does not reduce company value.

Today the scope of corporate citizenship touches every aspect of your business. Businesses operating in our global economy have become increasingly responsive to the demands of a range of stakeholders: communities, employees, customers, shareholders, and governments across the world. Many factors have contributed to this trend. The democratization of information and digital and social communication have been major factors. As more people have greater ability to communicate with and about companies across domestic and international borders, companies are held to account by greater numbers of stakeholders than ever before and as a result they are proactively managing their impacts.

DON'T MAKE THIS FUNDAMENTAL MISTAKE

Sometimes, executives think if their corporate citizenship initiatives are aligned too closely to their business strategy, their companies won't be viewed as good corporate citizens. They can sometimes confuse strategic alignment in this domain with the concept of "self-dealing" when a corporate citizenship program is both creating value by improving an aspect of the company and at the same time doing good in the world. Let's take a look at this assumption for a moment.

First ask yourself if the social or environmental good you achieve with your corporate citizenship investments is less good because your business may benefit also. A number of studies show consumers, employees, and other stakeholders respond much more positively to corporate citizenship initiatives that meet both the strategic needs of the company *and* create good in society.

This means the more logically connected your citizenship investments are to the operating context of your business, the more likely your customers are to accept that your company is committed to doing good. They do not have to work out why you're doing what you do, they just get it and give you credit for being a good corporate citizen.

IF YOU'RE STILL NOT CONVINCED ABOUT THE BENEFITS OF CONNECTING CORPORATE CITIZENSHIP AND BUSINESS STRATEGIES, READ THIS

You know now your corporate citizenship strategy should connect to, and support, the business strategy in your organization — taking into account your company's priorities, growth plan, location, expertise, and community needs. The strategy can be made up of a number of programs and investments across the social, environmental, and governance dimensions of your company's operations.

For the Boston College Center for Corporate Citizenship's 2017 *State of Corporate Citizenship* study, we talked to 750 executive respondents. Those who aligned their citizenship programs with their business objectives consistently reported increased success in achieving the outcomes valued by their companies (see Figure 1). Additional independent research also proves alignment and integration help companies achieve success with the following aims:

Figure 1: **Connecting Corporate Citizenship to Business Strategy. The 2017 BCCCC State of Corporate Citizenship study observed that companies that do not integrate corporate citizenship in their business strategy report achieving modest success in achieving business goals. However, companies that do integrate corporate citizenship in business strategy report significantly higher levels of success in achieving the business goals that they set for themselves**

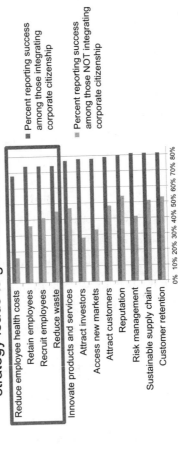

Connecting corporate citizenship to business strategy leads to great business success

- Reinforce their brand; deepen customer[7] and employee[8] involvement.

- Address environmental and social issues that have the potential to disrupt their business.[9]

- Assess the impact of their gifts because they understand they are closely related to their business experience.[10]

- Create reputational assets that contribute intangible value to the firm[11] while contributing to the common good.[12]

- Have philanthropic and other citizenship initiatives viewed as more credible as a result of logical connections to the purpose of the company.[13]

In the Boston College Center for Corporate Citizenship's *2015 Community Involvement Survey,* over 90% of companies that had connected their corporate citizenship strategy to their business strategy managed to reduce their employee health costs. This was compared with under 30% of businesses that had not. And 95% of businesses that connect their corporate citizenship strategy to their business strategy have improved their risk management, compared to only 55% of those that have not.

Given these results it's not surprising that for the first time in 30 years, executives predicted that the investment in corporate citizenship would increase over the next three years in every dimension queried, including human rights management, philanthropy, recycling, environmental investments, safe products, and employee volunteering.

Why the increased commitment? Because people are increasingly coming to understand corporate citizenship activity contributes to a company's success.

OVERCOMING BARRIERS TO STRATEGIC CORPORATE CITIZENSHIP

You'd think, given the statistics above, that every company would be implementing citizenship programs that connect to their business strategy. But as you've probably already discovered, there are many reasons why this doesn't happen. Much of this has to do with a lack of understanding about the true benefits that can be gained for both business and society.

Don't get us wrong — there are no 'bad' good actions. There are, however, some commonly misguided alternatives to pursuing a strategic approach:

- *Moral appeal*: "corporate citizenship should not be about benefiting the company; it should be about the company doing the right thing." This is a purely charitable motivation, and of course there's nothing wrong with it except that programs created with this aim are at risk of being seen as "extra"' because they have no connection to the firm's purpose or strategy.

- *License to operate*: if you're only considering what your community and stakeholders think about you right now, you're defining yourself by where you are today and not where you intend to be in the future.

- *Reputation management*: this confuses social, environmental, and business results with PR. Although there are clearly reputational benefits to good corporate citizenship, focusing purely on reputation leaves on the table other opportunities to create value.

You can see how these rationales focus on the *tension* between business and society, rather than on their *interdependence*. Rationales that aren't tied to the specific strategy of the company are not sufficient to help identify, prioritize, and address the social issues that matter most.

The more logically connected your corporate citizenship priorities are to your company's core business strategy, the more authentic and credible your program will be perceived by stakeholders of all types — customers, employees, shareholders, and community members — and the more value both your company and society will derive from the investment. This mutually reinforcing loop is a virtuous circle that creates not only a favorable business context, but also the world in which we want to live.

Integrating your corporate citizenship strategy with the vision and strategy of your company creates the basis for long-term success. This book helps you organize and communicate a clear plan.

From the Corner Office

With more than 30 years as an executive at the Walt Disney Company, Jay Rasulo shared his insights about effective corporate citizenship at one of the world's most beloved brands. Corporate citizenship lives through the actions of those it touches as they are inspired to imagine a better world and make the choices necessary to create it.

- Take the time to build a citizenship strategy that really links your company's brands and values with that effort.

- Focus and prioritize that linkage to your business's unique competitive advantage. When people understand the link between your organization, what it stands for, what it does, and the efforts that you make in the citizenship arena, it can not only be more impactful, but also will stick in their minds about who you are and what you do in this arena.

- Don't try to do too much all at once. Even in a large company, resources may be scarce, and the resource of time is always short. Set goals and targets — things that get measured get accomplished — and don't be afraid to adapt and change course along the way.

- Today's challenges are simply too big and too complex to solve as one individual or one group, or even one global company. The good news is that, in a hyperconnected society, businesses have an enormous opportunity to engage more people than ever before in social and philanthropic efforts.

Excerpted from Disney Senior Executive Vice President and Chief Financial Officer Jay Rasulo's March 24, 2014 speech at the Boston College Center 2014 International Corporate Citizenship Conference. Reprinted in The *Corporate Citizen* magazine, Issue 11, 2014.

CORPORATE CITIZENSHIP IN 10 STEPS

At the end of each chapter, you'll find a clear summary of the main points and a list of questions to ask your team. Ensuring that you and they have considered the questions — even if you haven't come to final resolution on some of them it will help to ensure that you have a fully integrated corporate citizenship program.

As we noted earlier in this chapter, "corporate citizenship" is called a lot of things; to avoid confusion, we're sticking to this one term throughout. Don't worry if your company calls it something different; the semantics aren't as important as what you're trying to achieve. Pick the terms that make the most sense for your culture and stick with them.

We all know that individuals doing good can make an impact, but with a whole *company*? How much more can you achieve if you harness the power of your entire corporation? The sooner you get started, the more quickly you can make change for the better, make a positive impact in the world, deliver top and bottom line results for your company, and build your corporate citizenship reputation at the same time.

NOTES

1. Orlitzky, Schmidt, and Rynes (2003).

2. Luo, Wang, Raithel, and Zheng (2015).

3. Margolis, Elfenbein, and Walsh (2007).

4. Flammer (2015).

5. Dimson, Karakaş, and Li (2015).

6. Delmas, Etzion, and Nairn-Birch (2013).

7. Gardberg and Fombrun (2006).

8. Vitaliano (2010).

9. Simmons and Becker-Olsen (2006).

10. Raffaelli and Glynn (2014).

11. KPMG AG Wirtschaftsprüfungsgesellschaft (2010).

12. Raithel, Wilczynski, Schloderer, and Schwaiger (2010).

13. Thomas, Fraedrich, and Mullen (2011).

SECTION 1

LAYING THE FOUNDATION AND GIVING YOUR TEAM THE RIGHT TOOLS

1

CONNECTING CORPORATE CITIZENSHIP TO BUSINESS PURPOSE

What's the purpose of your company? Stop and think about that for a moment. Perhaps your company has a "Mission" or "Vision," but purpose is different. Why was it originally created, even if that was many years ago? This can be an interesting question to ask and a difficult one to answer. There's a very good reason to make the effort. In the process of exploring these issues, you'll learn how to design a corporate citizenship strategy and program that is relevant, comprehensive, and — most importantly — that works.

All successful businesses were created originally to fill a market need or solve a societal problem. This is the core of purpose. The purpose of your company could have been to make life more convenient, to provide something essential, or even to create an exciting experience. Depending on how long your corporation has been around it may still be providing that same solution; alternatively, the company may now be selling products and services that address problems that did not exist at your founding with solutions that were unimaginable. At its core, a successful company delivers something to the world that only it can provide in its distinctive way. It's a special point of differentiation from its competitors. Purpose is the reason your company was created and exists today. It is related to vision and precedes strategy. When you have your company's core purpose clear, it should guide your corporate citizenship.

Let's look at some sample company websites to better understand the concept of purpose (Table 1).

The purposes of the example companies have changed relatively little over time. It's the *way* they realize their

Table 1: Company Business Purpose

This is the Company's Purpose	This is How They Realize Their Purpose
"3M is a global innovation company that never stops inventing."	"Over the years, our innovations have improved daily life for hundreds of millions of people all over the world. We have made driving at night easier, made buildings safer, and made consumer electronics lighter, less energy-intensive and less harmful to the environment. We even helped put a man on the moon."
"Campbell Soup Company's purpose: Real Food That Matters For Life's Moments."	"For generations, people have trusted Campbell to provide authentic, flavorful and readily available foods and beverages that connect them to each other, to warm memories, and to what's important today."
"McDonald's reaches customers with enjoyable meal experiences wherever they are."	"McDonald's is innovating new tastes and choices, while staying true to customer favorites. Modern service. Personal engagement. Great-tasting burgers and fries. Building on our commitments to our people, our communities, and our world."

purposes that have evolved, as their operating contexts have changed.

It's not always easy to uncover your core purpose, but if you get it right you'll have a solid foundation that provides the justification and boundaries for your business strategy and corporate citizenship program. What's more, unlocking a company's core purpose can unleash new ideas, helping you to think more imaginatively and broadly about how corporate citizenship contributes to your company's purpose and unique value proposition. Your company's purpose is here to stay, representing the value you provide to your customers year after year. It's not a program or a campaign, it's for life.

For example, think about Ford Motor Co. The business was originally created to provide affordable transport for everyday people, and it still does that today. Ford changed its business model to adapt, like all companies do. It went from mass-producing a single model in a single color to customizing individual models and features and vehicle types (sedans, coupes, trucks, hybrids). In today's sharing economy some consumers either can't afford or aren't interested in owning a car, but they still want to be able to use one from time to time. So Ford has developed partnerships with technology companies and now leases vehicles to ride-sharing systems as well as selling them to individual owners. The company is still true to its original purpose of giving people an affordable way to travel from place to place, just not in exactly the same way it used to. Ford used an advertisement in the 2017 Super Bowl to help remind consumers about its broad mobility purpose.

We mentioned McDonald's in our examples above. Their original purpose was to serve fast, family-friendly meals on the go, to the increasingly mobile society of mid-century America. When McDonald's was founded people ate out less, mainly at lunch and dinner; McDonald's therefore came up with the solution of burgers and fries. They've interpreted that purpose across both decades and geographic regions. As work hours became longer and more women worked outside the home there was higher demand for meals on the go at different times of day, so McDonald's developed a popular breakfast menu and expanded its service hours. In the United States, the breakfast menu is so popular that McDonald's now serves breakfast all day. McDonald's expects to have more than 450 restaurants in India by 2020,[1] and none of them serve beef. You can see how they've interpreted their purpose through a changing context and applied their core competencies (replicable inventory and fast, easy preparation) to new contexts; if they had thought about their company purpose as "getting customers fast burgers," they wouldn't have had the flexibility to apply these skills to changing times and environments.

After all, in the 1950s and 1960s, "fast, affordable, family-friendly meals on the go" was defined very differently to how they are today. In those days delivering hot, tasty, and consistent burgers and fries from clean stores, being supportive of the community with gifts in kind, and supporting the local little leagues were sufficient to fulfill their purpose. But as consumer expectations changed over time and geography, and as their business grew, McDonald's had to maintain their core competencies in menu planning, purchasing, and training, and add new ones in nutrition, wellness, and environmentally friendly packaging. Now they have wellness initiatives for families to understand better the nutritional profiles of their menu items and offer training and development to employees (Warren Buffett has called the company a gateway to future employment). Their commitments have changed as their context has changed, but their purpose has not.

BUSINESS PURPOSE, VISION, AND STRATEGY

By the way, if you're wondering what the difference is between a company's purpose, vision, and strategy, it's this: purpose is the motivation for all it does; vision is a vivid, easily communicated image for how the world will be different if it's successful in achieving its objectives; and strategy is the plan of action for how it will compete in the market to achieve this vision. Purpose is the reason you're undertaking your strategy, and usually doesn't change. Purpose informs decision-making and promotes systems thinking. Strategy changes as customers, consumers, and markets evolve. Later on, we'll look at strategy in more detail; for now, just know that it springs from your corporate purpose. One of your key jobs as a corporate leader is to set the vision for where the company will go and to communicate it in ways that inspire action among your people. The behaviors that you reward — both what is done and how it is done — establish the culture of your company.

HOW DOES YOUR CORPORATE CITIZENSHIP PROGRAM SUPPORT YOUR COMPANY'S PURPOSE AND STRATEGY?

Your company has a core purpose, and so does your corporate citizenship program. Can you describe what it is? How would your company's customers describe it? What would your employees say about it? How about your suppliers, investors, and other stakeholders?

You can sit in your office and ruminate on this, or you can tap into the wisdom of your team. Ask what success would look like for them. Their words are important here, as they will likely use different terminology than you. A subordinate might say, "I love coming to work because what this company is doing is making a real impact." An investor on Wall Street would never say, "Well, it's great they have a robust volunteer program." They may, however, note your company has a low staff turnover and does a great job of managing its people. Does your corporate citizenship investment contribute to that strength? Data tell us there is a strong positive correlation of volunteerism and employee engagement with low turnover, so you probably do contribute to the Wall Street investor's assessments of the quality of management and stability of the company.[2]

To inspire people you need to paint a vivid picture of your corporate citizenship strategy, and how you intend to fulfill and measure it. At this stage, you're simply collecting information; imagine you have a pile of "corporate purpose" on your desk and a stack of "what I'm going to do about it." You also have a collection of words and images to describe your purpose to the people that matter your team, your board, your customers, your suppliers, your community.

From the Corner Office

The best corporate citizenship programs reflect the vision and mission of the company, and executives are uniquely qualified to arrange this alignment. At New Balance, president and chief executive officer Rob DeMartini, ensures that all initiatives, corporate citizenship or otherwise, tie in with company values.

Linking corporate citizenship to core business strategies yields results. The best organizations lead with their values. They take the long view. Our values — teamwork, integrity, and total customer satisfaction — are our guideposts.

We want to be successful — but not at any cost. We'll be successful on our terms, with Responsible Leadership. When the choice is between right and right now, the most successful organizations choose right based on a set of core values deeply held in the C-suite, through every associate down to the factory floor.

Business is a powerful force for social change. It is the role of Responsible Leadership to lead the way.

New Balance President and CEO, **Rob DeMartini**

From *The Corporate Citizen* magazine, Issue 11, 2014.

WHAT MAKES YOUR COMPANY UNIQUE?

Remember when we talked about what makes your company different and special at the beginning of this chapter? You may have wondered what this means for the corporation you lead.

There are thousands of service companies, hundreds of food companies, and dozens of automotive companies and airlines, but it's what they each do differently from the others that gives them their competitive advantage — their differentiation. Are products offered faster? Are they more innovative? Do they offer unique or more features? Are they less expensive than competitors? It's not just *what* they provide but it's *how*!

What makes your product or service special? If you're a retailer, you may describe your stores as the most welcoming place in the world to shop for high-end goods. Your shoes may be the ultimate in low-priced but high-fashioned items — or you may employ a buy-a-pair/give-a-pair strategy. To determine what makes you unique sounds simple but it can be really hard to answer; even large leadership teams sometimes have a difficult time answering this question.

HOW DO YOU DIFFERENTIATE YOUR CORPORATE CITIZENSHIP PROGRAM?

Maybe you have the best R&D people in the world, or possibly your ability to deliver a particular experience is second to none. These are your firm's core competencies — the things you do exceptionally well as a business and which differentiate you from your competitors. Your purpose and your competencies come together to make up your value proposition. Understanding how your unique value proposition intersects a clear societal need is the key to unlocking measureable outcomes and impact (**Figure 2**). And just like with your purpose, you now need to be able to describe your complete value proposition so that anyone in the company would say, "Oh yes, that sounds just like [your company name]." They get it. They understand what you deliver and what you do in a more unique and compelling way than anyone else.

MAPPING YOUR BUSINESS PROCESS FLOW

In order to define the corporate citizenship building blocks, tactics, risks, opportunities, and link to strategy, you need to think about the flow — or value chain — of your business. From a corporate citizenship perspective, every element in this flow will illuminate opportunities and challenges. These line and support functions could have human rights implications, environmental impacts, activism issues, or energy and water requirements. When you look at the business flow, you'll find the levers you can pull to create or enhance your citizenship program. There may be too many to include in the first pass, although by mapping it out you're uncovering the risks as well as the opportunities for your work. We will cover many key business functions in the following chapters, but this effort is more than an intellectual exercise.

Figure 2: A Strategic "Sweet-Spot" Exists for Your Enterprise to Deliver Differentiated Business Results and Social Impact. Competitive and reputational advantage exists where your core competencies overlap a compelling environmental or social opportunity and the ability to measure or monetize that impact

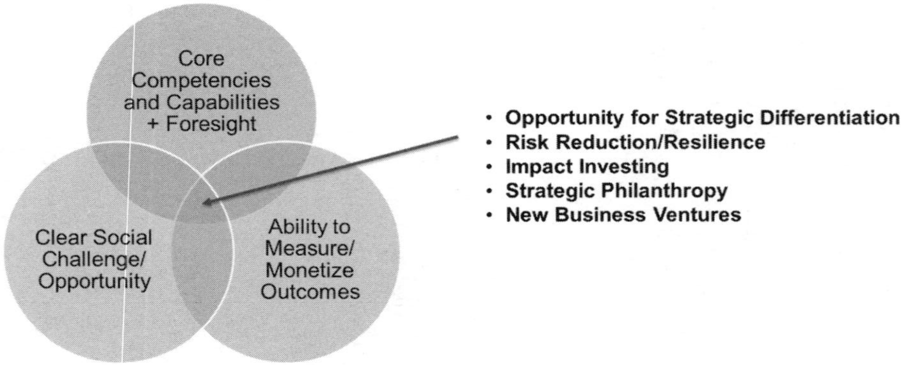

Core Competencies and Capabilities + Foresight

Ability to Measure/ Monetize Outcomes

Clear Social Challenge/ Opportunity

- **Opportunity for Strategic Differentiation**
- **Risk Reduction/Resilience**
- **Impact Investing**
- **Strategic Philanthropy**
- **New Business Ventures**

The deeper the examination of your business processes, the more value you will unlock.

YOUR COMPETITION

You've considered your company's purpose, vision, strategy, processes, core competencies, employees, and customers. Before you move forward, you need to look at your competition again from the corporate citizenship perspective.

You may think of competitors as businesses competing in the same product or service sector as your own, but there are many different ways to compete. It's especially important to define your competition according to the key risks and opportunities in your business. For instance, there may be risks and opportunities in your supply chain which you've positioned yourself to deal with differently than your competitors. Or you might have some unique competitive advantage or disadvantage in distribution, sales, or communications.

From a business perspective alone, never mind corporate citizenship, you could be competing with almost anyone. If your company wants to recruit the best and brightest employees, you can become better at recruiting by creating an engaging, inspiring workplace. When you know who you compete with — and in what arenas — you've begun to build a framework to differentiate your corporation from the competition.

From a corporate citizenship perspective, you could have a competitor outside of your sector because they're competing with you on the ethical nature of their supply chain. It's also important to consider your competition from the standpoint of reputation. If you were to walk around your local community and ask people who your competitors were, they might say the local hospital, university, or nonprofit, because they're viewing you all as members of a single community rather than as members of disparate industries. If you are asking financial analysts about your competitive set, they will likely be assessing you against companies in the same industry, offering the same (or similar) services. If you are asking your HR leaders, they will be looking at companies across industries (and very likely geographies) to attract the best talent possible to your company. Understanding who your various stakeholders view as competitors is an important undertaking.

10 QUESTIONS TO ASK YOUR TEAM BEFORE YOU MOVE ON

1. What is the core purpose of our business? Do we know how our customers, and society in general, would describe it?

2. Can we describe what long-term success looks like for our business? Is this view understood across your organization?

3. Does our vision of success paint a picture, describe a feeling, and evoke value for our employees, customers, and other stakeholders?

4. Have we mapped out our business processes and assessed them for risk and opportunity?

5. Have we identified elements of our current or planned corporate citizenship program that can help mitigate risks or achieve opportunities?

6. What are our company's core competencies (what it does better than any other company on the planet)?

7. Are we exploiting our core competencies in your corporate citizenship? Or are we running a "me too" program?

8. Can we identify elements of our corporate citizenship program that do not connect to our purpose and/or core competencies? How might we reallocate the resources that these efforts consume?

9. Do we know who our competition is within both industry and reputation contexts?

10. Do we know how we compare to each competitor in each context?

NOTES

1. http://www.thehindu.com/business/mcdonalds-india-to-double-outlets-by-2020/article7648207.ece

2. The Boston College Center for Corporate Citizenship (2015).

2

CREATING ADVANTAGE IN YOUR MARKETPLACE

Now that we've looked at business purpose, let's turn to the marketplace. Corporate citizenship is very much about building relationships, and there are many interested parties who seek to influence what you're doing. The more effectively you engage with these stakeholders, the more leverage you will have with them as you implement your corporate citizenship strategy.

We'll look at customers, activists, employees, and investors, as these are groups you'll need to understand and engage with if you want to be an influential player in the corporate citizenship space. Employees are a particularly important stakeholder group. We'll talk more specifically about them in Chapter 3.

CREATING ADVANTAGE WITH YOUR PRODUCTS AND SERVICES

Your initial step is to clearly identify your customers, and then to prioritize them. Not all customers are created

From the Corner Office

It is important to keep in mind that corporate citizenship efforts should not be separate from the business, or even simply run parallel to business objectives.

Instead, environmental and social efforts can complement those of the business — strengthening customer relationships and improving the product — as they do at Campbell Soup Company.

> At Campbell, we are addressing a unique range of topics through our citizenship programs, including sustainable agriculture, responsible sourcing, promotion of sound nutrition, and responsiveness to consumers' expectations of the foods that they choose for themselves and their families.
>
> Of all the activities that an organization undertakes, it is corporate social responsibility that humanizes, civilizes, and personalizes the competitive world of global commerce. This is hard and important work.
>
> As the leader of Campbell, I believe that we can make a profit and make a difference. It has been our legacy for 145 years and it is our future.

Campbell Soup Company President and CEO, **Denise Morrison**

From *The Corporate Citizen* magazine, Issue 11, 2014.

equally; some have more value to you than others. You might also have strategic partners, or customers you're trying to grow from small to large. Consider your key customers or customer segments and create a prioritized list. You could base this on size or influence, although you might also consider factors such as geographic areas where your business wants to expand, customers who are growing the fastest, or even customers who best align with your strategic focus.

HOW CUSTOMERS RELATE TO WHAT YOU PRODUCE OR PROVIDE

The products and services you sell have an impact on society far wider than their actual usage. This ranges from the actual impact (the environmental, human, or societal impacts of what your company produces) and the perceived or realized impact (views held by your customers and consumers).

If you're a manufacturer, this impact is tangible, and you can see it playing out every day all across the world. Sugar taxes imposed on soft drinks in various countries and the debate about whether advanced pharmaceutical drugs should be made available in undeveloped countries are just two examples of how products are not just products in customers' eyes — they are bundles of ethical and cost issues. This presents both challenges and opportunities for you. Rethinking how you source and deliver products can lead to a host of different ways to approach things.

For decades, the performance regulations companies had to deal within the corporate citizenship space were all "you shall not" — you shall not emit so many pounds of this and you shall not dispose of so many tons of that.

In recent years, the worlds of regulation and voluntary standards have moved toward a disclosure mindset — in other words, to be competitive, businesses are expected to provide customers — and sometimes the general public — with information so that they can make their own purchase or "enforcement" decisions. The era of "radical transparency" is here for all companies.

WHAT DOESN'T KILL YOU MAKES YOU STRONGER: WORKING WITH CHALLENGING STAKEHOLDERS

So who are your stakeholders? They're groups such as suppliers, customers, and employees. You can also add external groups such as competitors, members of the communities where you operate, values-based investors, issues advocates, regulators, activist groups, and policy makers.

Most large companies attract a wide range of advocates, activists, and values-based investors (more about the investors below). There's a widely used acronym which covers most of their areas of interest: environmental, social, and governance (ESG). Historically, the first impulse of business people, at least in the United States, has been to dismiss stakeholders with ESG concerns as antibusiness, antimarket, antiprogress socialists who don't understand the power and importance of market forces. This response represents a lost opportunity, because if you dismiss the chance to hear from your non-financial stakeholders, you can't learn from them. In today's world of citizen journalism and social media, thinking of those who call for accountability from institutions as fringe is no longer practical. These stakeholder groups can gain traction and support quickly.

Ask yourself, what issues are most important to each of these stakeholders? You probably have a sense about the most pressing issues in your marketplace already. However, different stakeholders will have different priorities. Many are single-issue-focused organizations we would normally think of as activists, or advocates for a cause. They wake up in the morning and it's deforestation; they go to bed at night and the issue is still deforestation. Every time you talk with them, it's always about deforestation. So while you're trying to manage multiple issues from a corporate citizenship perspective, they're trying to get you to focus on *their* one thing. They may have had a relationship with your business based on that single topic for many years, and while they may sometimes be challenging to work with they can also be the most helpful in identifying how their issue will impact your business long term.

If you want to be a leader in corporate citizenship you don't just need to manage this process, you need to *leverage* it, so you're the best in your sector — even the world. You need to create a competitive advantage out of the thing that looks like trouble to other companies. Engaging these groups can also enhance the work your company or industry association is doing to establish norms and standards of practice to address complex social and environmental issues such as sustainable consumption and climate change.

IF YOU CAN'T DIFFERENTIATE, COLLABORATE

Sometimes it does not make sense to forge ahead alone to lead the pack due to lack of resources, expertise, or executive buy-in. Other times you may have missed the leadership position on a particular issue that will continue to be material to your business operations. In those cases, it is often better to collaborate with others in your industry to address the issue through tactics including voluntary standards, codes of conduct, supplier training, and others. This is sometimes referred to as pre-competitive "collabotition" or the practice of collaboration with competitors to achieve mutually held objectives. Industry organizations like the Electronic Industry Citizenship Coalition (EICC), the Roundtable on Sustainable Palm Oil (RSPO), and many others that work with industries such as the Forestry Stewardship Council (FSC) exist to help companies work through issues material to the whole industry efficiently.

MANAGING THE PROCESS

To get started, have your team create a list of your main stakeholders, identify their potential issues relative to your company, and then create a list of priority issues. You could organize it by topic, functions in your business, or regulatory changes happening around the world that could potentially have a negative impact on your business. Are there developments in Asia, for instance, that could be an early warning of what could happen in your country, or vice versa? In Europe, genetically modified organisms (GMOs) were required to be labeled long before the United States, so this is an example of a change in one geographical area that diffuses to another market. Large companies operate globally and what happens in the European Union is likely a precursor to what happens elsewhere. For example, starting in 2017,[1] EU Directive 2014/95 affects any company or organization (undertaking) operating in an EU member state with the following attributes:

- More than 500 employees;

- Are "public interest" organizations, which are defined to include EU exchange-listed companies as well as some unlisted companies, such as credit institutions, insurance undertakings, and other businesses selected by Member States (based on size, number of employees, and/or activities);

- A balance sheet total of at least EUR$20 million (approximately US$25 million) or a net turnover of at least EUR$40 million (approximately US$50 million).

This directive requires that all member states establish guidelines for disclosures on sustainability of social and environmental factors, with a view to identifying sustainability risks and increasing investor and consumer trust. The EU Directive is intended to provide sufficient level of comparability to meet the needs of investors and other stakeholders as well as the need to provide consumers with easy access to information on the impact of businesses on society. This push toward transparency will certainly have an effect on the disclosure practices of companies all over the world.

When do you expect these issues to become business-relevant, and how could they impact your business and customers? We'll look at process for tracking stakeholders and issues in Chapters 3 and 4.

CREATING ADVANTAGE BY WORKING WITH VALUES-SCREENED INVESTORS

Investors in your business come in many shapes and sizes — institutional, private, socially responsible, values-based, and ethical. It's the larger institutional investors with a socially responsible ethos we'll focus on here. As a group they file hundreds of shareowner resolutions each year related to ESG topics. These resolutions demand better disclosure of corporate activities that run the gamut ranging from political contributions, environmental or supply chain activities, remuneration, or governance structures and practices just to name a few topics. Investors may ask whether there's sufficient gender or racial diversity on your corporation's board, or how easy you make it for shareowners to access board meetings. In recent years, these proposals have been gaining a lot of traction as well as higher vote tallies.

Just as with issues-based activists, so it is with values-based investors. If you're not paying attention to them, you'll not be managing a relationship, and you will potentially be responding to a resolution.

With this in mind, almost every large company has adopted a strategy to engage with large values-screened investors and analysts on a periodic basis. Intel was one of the first companies to do this formally back in 1998, which resulted in it earning recognition and credibility with social investors. As a result, by 2003 Intel stock had become the largest holding in socially responsible mutual funds in the world.[2] Why did Intel go to all this trouble? Because these values-based investors see a high level of ESG performance as indicative of a company's long-term success, engaging with them meant that Intel could build a win–win relationship. Values-based investors can often serve like your external partners from a corporate citizenship perspective. They care not only about the financial success of your business, but also about the long-term environmental, social, and governance assets of your company.

A recent notable instance of this came when Larry Fink, CEO of investment company BlackRock, wrote in February of 2016 to the CEOs of BlackRock's portfolio companies to assert the need for better long-term thinking among corporate executives. As the CEO of one of the largest asset management companies in the world, Fink's letter earned wide media attention. Among the topics he covered in the letter,

> *Generating sustainable returns over time requires a sharper focus not only on governance, but also on environmental and social factors facing companies today. These issues offer both risks and opportunities, but for too long, companies have not considered them core to their business — even*

when the world's political leaders are increasingly focused on them, as demonstrated by the Paris Climate Accord. Over the long-term, environmental, social and governance (ESG) issues — ranging from climate change to diversity to board effectiveness — have real and quantifiable financial impacts.[3]

His 2017 letter focused, in part, on the need for more long-term thinking in business and the rationale for addressing uneven wage growth to ensure broader economic participation.[4]

So how can *you* replicate Intel's success? Set up a scheduled meeting, just like we talked about with the activists, but this time between yourselves and the investor groups that are focused on environmental or social governance. Your aim is to educate them about what you're doing and listen to their concerns. Intel found that this process created significant trust and also generated a wealth of information and market intelligence which helped inform their future strategy.

10 QUESTIONS TO ASK YOUR TEAM BEFORE YOU MOVE ON

1. Have we identified our key customers either by importance of relationship, importance to our business, or influence over our success?

2. Have we identified other key stakeholders? Have we identified and do we understand their key issues?

3. Who is responsible for monitoring, communicating, and managing emerging issues within our company? Do we have a process for doing so?

4. Have we sought out activists who either have a negative opinion of us, or want us to change some aspect of what we do?

5. If we are a publicly traded company, do we understand who our shareowners are and how values-based investors factor into our investor holdings?

6. Have we started to monitor shareowner resolutions of ESG issues that could affect our business? How are we using this information to our advantage?

7. Do we understand the impact of disclosure-based regulations or transparency in general on our business?

8. What are our customers' key corporate citizenship concerns? What are we doing to help advance them?

9. How are we working with our own suppliers in order to advance our corporate citizenship agenda?

10. What are we asking our suppliers to do or not do, in order to advance our customers' ESG priorities?

NOTES

1. EU Directive 2014/95.

2. *Research Magazine* (2003), Intel Corporation (2004).

3. *New York Times* (2016).

4. http://www.cnbc.com/2017/01/24/blackrocks-larry-finks-warning-to-s-and-p-ceos.html. Accessed on April 7, 2017.

3

OF THE PEOPLE, FOR THE PEOPLE, BY THE PEOPLE

All of the people you rely upon for business success — both inside and outside of your company — are your stakeholders, which we define as any group or ecosystem that can impact or be impacted by your business.

STAKEHOLDERS ARE THE REASON CORPORATE CITIZENSHIP PROGRAMS CAN'T BE A ONE-SIZE-FITS-ALL

Stakeholders exist in a hierarchy. One of the most well-established sustainability decision-making frameworks recognized this hierarchy: we must have a healthy environment to have a healthy society; we must have a healthy society to have a healthy economy.[1] Environment enables society. Society enables economy. They are not distinct, but rather interoperable and hierarchical. The interoperability of environment, society, and economy are shown in **Figure 3a. Figure 3b** illustrates the nested relationship of these domains.

Figure 3: Spheres of Sustainability

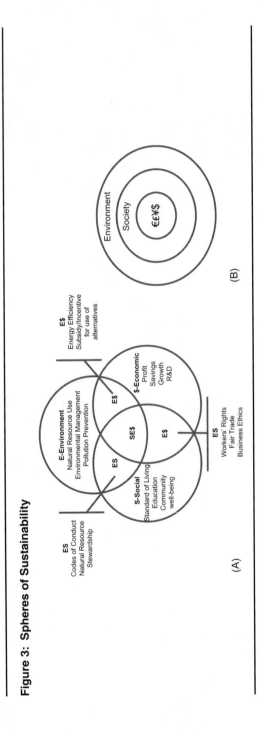

Think of your stakeholders as an anchor point, the context for your corporate citizenship program. Everything starts with them — and your stakeholders are not only individuals, but also include the environment and its ecosystem services on which we depend to live, multiple sectors of our society, and of course, customers, employees, and the myriad others upon whom we depend to maintain a successful business.

HOW YOUR CORPORATE CITIZENSHIP PROGRAM CAN AFFECT YOUR STAKEHOLDERS

Companies often overlook that they have capabilities that are distinctive to them, through which they can positively impact a social or environmental problem in ways no other company can.

One example is The Disney Channel. Disney has an enormous media footprint, especially with kids and families. So they've started working with evidence-based messaging targeted at kids, for causes like reducing bullying or improving body image and confidence for young girls. This has included developing story lines in their network TV programs about how it's ok to be an individual (so the top line message isn't necessarily about bullying, it's a subtler message about respecting differences). These themes run through all of their "tween" programming. They are embedded in story lines and encourage children to celebrate their individual strengths and to stand up for what they think is right. The message is clear: the brave and heroic thing to do is to be kind and accept each other's individuality.

From the Corner Office

State Street is one of the largest financial institutions in the world with $27 trillion in custody and $2 trillion under management. In addition to delivering important ESG outcomes, effective corporate citizenship creates lasting business value. That's why at State Street, corporate citizenship is considered essential.

> *Being socially responsible is both a moral and business imperative. Any company that doesn't strive to be a good corporate citizen risks undermining its reputation and jeopardizing its profitability over the long run.*
>
> *Employees, customers, shareholders, and other stakeholders want to work for, do business with, and invest in companies that take their social responsibilities seriously and have a positive impact on the world.*
>
> **In addition to more satisfied stakeholders, corporate responsibility makes for stronger communities and better economic growth prospects.**
>
> *For these reasons and many more, corporate citizenship is not just the right thing to do; it's the smart thing to do.*

State Street Chairman and Chief Executive Officer, **Jay Hooley**

From *The Corporate Citizen* magazine, Issue 12, 2015.

In this way, the Disney Channel's corporate citizenship program is having a positive effect on children and on society as a whole — not only in their environmental commitments and philanthropy and employee programs, but also through their programming. And the benefit for Disney is enhanced brand value, as parents and children respect it all the more for these positive messages.

Always look for opportunities not only to receive good from your stakeholders, but also to do good for them. There are many ways to implement projects that may not bring short-term benefit, but provide natural opportunities for you to do good in the course of your "regularly scheduled programming" as Disney has demonstrated. In the long run, they'll add to your company's reputation and relationship with your customers and other interested stakeholders.

STAKEHOLDERS BEFORE ISSUES

When determining which issues to focus on, it might seem like corporate citizenship professionals should start with the hot topics.

What could go wrong if you were to focus on hot issues not aligned with stakeholder interests? You might find yourself being influenced by issues getting the most public attention right now, but which are not necessarily the ones most meaningful for your stakeholders or business strategy. You could run the risk of investing in programs that aren't positively impacting the people you're most concerned about, or the contexts you're most trying to influence.

All stakeholders are not created equal, in that some groups have a greater ability to influence (or be influenced by) your actions and program. Stakeholders may rise or fall in importance over time. Prioritizing stakeholders and issues is a continuous process. Relationships and issues shift over time, and a group that was not as influential or whose issues were not as urgent yesterday may change position (seemingly overnight if you're not monitoring all the time). Your team should establish a discipline of review to assess:

- *Legitimacy*: How great is your impact on that group or resources that they need? How valid are their arguments and demands?

- *Influence*: How capable is this stakeholder of affecting your program?

- *Urgency*: What is the degree to which stakeholder claims call for immediate attention?

We've adapted the model developed by Ronald Mitchell to reflect the process by which we think stakeholders should be prioritized today. Those stakeholders that have a legitimate claim on your business — those who are impacted most by your operation and/or on whom you depend to make your business successful — should get priority attention. Those who have influence are prioritized as a group to watch and stay in touch. This group is tricky to manage as they possess some power that may allow them to affect your operating environment. Those who have urgent issues — which may or may not relate to your business but whom you could help — would be prioritized next. Think here about

From the Corner office

Making it work around the world: Global Program, local strategy

So your organization has started its global Citizenship program, reached out to internal and external stakeholders, conducted materiality testing, and determined priorities based upon the results of the testing. The next step is the hardest putting those priorities into action through a strategic planning process. This is a challenging process for any organization, but is even more complex for a regional affiliate of a multinational diversified company like the one for which I work. Several things should be considered.

Have you done a local or divisional materiality test? While results normally should be consistent with the global ones, variations can help shape a local strategic plan. For example, volunteerism in many countries is not as developed as it is in the United States and may not show as a priority on a global scale. This may be extremely important for your employee stakeholders and may only show up on a local survey and would need to be built into your strategy.

Community engagement is typically a significant aspect of most citizenship platforms, but in a geographically diverse enterprise, community needs cannot easily be addressed by a global strategy except in a very general way. Local strategic planning really needs to do a "deep dive" into each community and its needs. My company operates in poor rural areas as well as some of the wealthiest communities and strategy needs to reflect the difference in needs of these diverse environments.

Imagine that it has been determined that your global priority for the environment is the reduction of use of water in the manufacturing process and that you work in a country where there is limited manufacturing. How do you define an approach for your environmental initiatives that is consistent with the global program? Here is where the local needs will deviate from global priorities. Global colleagues must be flexible and understand that the environment may be important to local stakeholders, but not necessarily in the same way, and they need to be tolerant of a different approach. Materiality testing can be critical in demonstrating to global colleagues the need to take a different direction at the affiliate level.

I think that we can all agree on the importance of having well-defined global priorities that can be used as a basis for local strategy in order to allow for greater focus, clarity in communications, demonstrating impact and for measuring progress for social reporting. It is however incumbent on those of us located in a region or division to know and understand what is unique for our stakeholders and to develop a nuanced approach shaped to those needs.

Sanofi U.S. Vice President of Corporate Social Responsibility, **John Spinnato**

communities affected by natural disasters. Any community affected by natural disasters will have urgent needs. If the community affected is not among your arenas of operation or markets, you might limit your level of support because that particular event is urgent, but does not legitimately connect to your business. Those who possess more than one of the attributes described above should get higher levels of attention depending on the combination of attributes.

There are so many issues in the world today and so many stakeholders who are advocating for worthy causes, that you need a way to prioritize which you can target for attention. In our experience, the most efficient way to prioritize issues is to think first about the stakeholders. Issues belong to stakeholders and if the stakeholder is important to you, it is likely that their issues will be too.

Take a minute to prioritize your stakeholders. Here are some examples of how stakeholders might be prioritized based on their attributes.

Legitimacy, Urgency, Influence = 7 (if you are a consumer brand, consumers with concerns about ingredients who have the attention of media or another significant communications platform like social media might fall here)

Legitimacy, Influence = 6 (executives with specific priorities, standards organizations, or codes of conduct organizations might be prioritized at this level)

Legitimacy, Urgency = 5 (if you are a consumer brand, consumers with concerns about ingredients or supply chain issues, but with no access to key players in the industry or media might fall here)

Influence, Urgency = 4 (well-organized non-governmental organizations (NGOs) with specific campaigns that have low connection to your business might be prioritized at this level)

Legitimacy = 3 (suppliers who contribute to the creation of your product or service would have a minimum ranking at this level — it can rise at any time with the addition of another attribute, but it will not fall)

Influence = 2 (general interest media might fall here, as might executive colleagues)

Urgency = 1 (smaller or unrelated advocacy groups that have significant issue concerns unrelated to your business would fall here)

Looking at **Figure 4,** you can see that those stakeholders who have the most legitimate concerns about how your company may be impacting them, followed by those who are influential, or whose issues are urgent. Influence does not necessarily confer legitimacy, but it may merit attention, for example. Those stakeholders with multiple attributes will require more attention. You can prioritize your engagement with stakeholders based

---

Figure 4: Stakeholder Prioritization

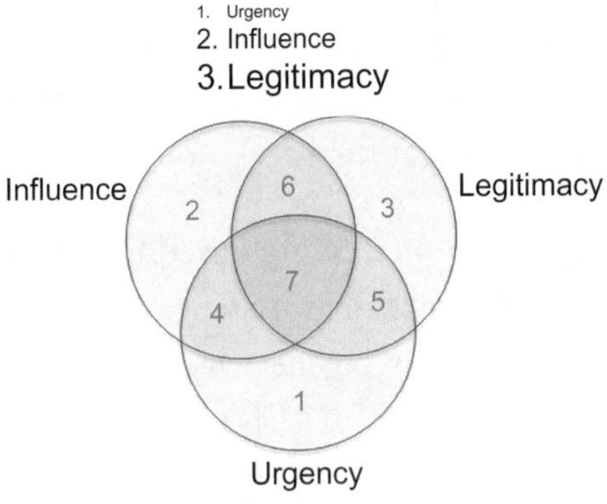

1. Urgency
2. Influence
3. Legitimacy

Influence   Legitimacy

Urgency

Source: This figure is adapted from Mitchell et al. (1997).

on the degrees to which they possess these attributes. Once you have mapped your stakeholders, you can plan your responses to their concerns.

KEEP SCANNING THE HORIZON

Although we've talked about the importance of not jumping too fast into the hot issues, you do need to know what's happening on the issues landscape as a whole. McDonalds could never have adapted its corporate citizenship strategies so effectively over time if it had not been aware of what was happening in the media, social, health, and environmental arenas. For instance, in 1995, 75% of all media articles about obesity focused on it as an issue of personal responsibility rather than corporate responsibility. Over the next five years, this number was completely inverted, with 75% of the responsibility being shouldered by food and drink corporations.[2] These articles had a direct impact on McDonalds' customers, which meant they needed to take action. And they did.

After you have identified your stakeholder groups, make note of the issues that you know or suspect to be of concern. You can now begin to map these onto a materiality matrix in the areas that correlate to their ranking. You can move them up or down a bit based on the likelihood that the concern will materialize — and the severity of the issue if it does. Use your judgment. This is art and science and remember that the stakeholders and their issues can and will move over time.

Figure 5 shows one way of mapping social and environmental issues of greatest concern to stakeholders and

Figure 5: Issue Management

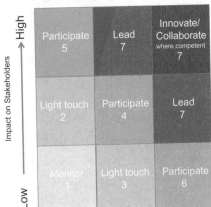

Notes: Use this framework as a way to prioritize the issues that your stakeholders are concerned with and that affect your company. This model provides a way for thinking about how much effort and resource you will allocate to specific issue.

your business. On the Y-axis is the issue's impact on stakeholders, low to high. The X-axis shows the impact of the issue on your business. Those in the upper right hand are those you've identified as most important; these are the issues in which you would devote significant resources to addressing. At the highest level of engagement, your company will be working with stakeholder groups collaboratively and applying your core competence to develop solutions to pressing environmental and social problems. You can also create an incredibly helpful feedback loop. By identifying the right stakeholders, you get feedback from a group of people who matter to you, so you're able to understand their expectations of your company. You're also more likely to stick with this

From the Corner Office

Microsoft works to better the world by revolutionizing the ways in which people interact with it. During the company's 2014 Annual Shareholder Meeting, CEO Satya Nadella revealed one crucial key to success.

> *Diversity and inclusiveness is a critical topic for our time, for our industry, for Microsoft and it's important to have candid conversation and, most importantly, robust action. Since 2006, we have transparently disclosed demographic (employee) data. This helps us internally to both talk about diversity and inclusion and galvanize for action. We are focused on ensuring that Microsoft will be the best place to work for smart, curious people across cultures, genders, ethnicities, and lifestyles. Our commitments:*

- *Equal opportunity and equal pay for equal work*
- *Develop a diverse talent base in Microsoft, and retain them as they grow*
- *A culture of inclusiveness*

> *The business case for inclusiveness is clear. The sensibility that is required in order to build products that are loved by diverse groups of people is not going to be possible if you don't have diversity in the workforce ... I am excited about our future, and confident that we have the ambition, vision, and talent to deliver the innovation that will touch every individual and every organization in every corner of the globe.*

Microsoft Corporation Chief Executive Officer, **Satya Nadella**

From *The Corporate Citizen* magazine, Issue 12, 2015.

relationship for a longer period of time. When you work with these people over time and stay focused on issues that affect them long term, your corporate citizenship initiatives are seen as more credible, by this group as well as others in your organization. This improves relationships with your customers, your employees, and your managers. You and your company are seen as authentic.

Don't ignore the people in the lower left-hand quadrant, who you know have both a low likelihood of being impacted by your corporate citizenship program *and* low influence over it. Instead, keep an eye on them and monitor over time. As your company's context changes, they might start to move into the upper right corner of the quadrant. You don't need to engage with them now, you just need to stay aware.

YOUR MOST IMPORTANT STAKEHOLDER GROUP

One final note: the most vital group is your company's employees. A huge part of what most corporations want to achieve today is a stable, productive workforce with low turnover, and that's a big challenge. Your HR department should be involved with your corporate citizenship team to develop programs that will help with employee engagement, productivity, and recruitment, and improve the reputation of the company as a positive force in the community. In our experience, this key relationship is often under-leveraged.

10 QUESTIONS TO ASK YOUR TEAM BEFORE YOU MOVE ON

1. Have we identified our key stakeholders and do we understand which have the greatest impact on our company and are most important to our corporate citizenship program?

2. Do we understand which stakeholders are most impacted by our company and how our corporate citizenship program could address their concerns?

3. Do we know how our stakeholders interact with each other?

4. Have we created a matrix or mapped out the issues most important to them?

5. What do we want each of these stakeholders to know about our company and what do we want them do to act on that information?

6. Do we know what our employees care about the most — does it vary by generation or geographic location?

7. How might these issues change over time?

8. What are the inherent risks and opportunities that lie within our stakeholder groups?

9. What timeframe is reasonable to monitor our stakeholder landscape?

10. How is our HR department engaging employees with our corporate citizenship commitments?

NOTES

1. EPA Sustainability Concepts in Decision-Making: Tools and Approaches for the US Environmental Protection Agency 2012, p. 26.

2. Lawrence (2004).

4

CONNECTING CORPORATE CITIZENSHIP TO BUSINESS STRATEGY

Strategy without tactics is the slowest route to victory. Tactics without strategy is the noise before defeat.

SunTzu in *The Art of War*

As an executive leader at your company, it is given that you are thinking about your business strategy all day, every day. For those who are more objective-focused, this may not be the case. They are thinking about the tasks they must complete. One of your key jobs as an executive leader is to remind everyone in the company from the highest most strategically focused, through all of the levels of implementation about your business objectives and how the successful completion of their tasks will help to achieve those objectives. Corporate citizenship programs should advance this purpose also. Corporate citizenship and business strategy should be closely inter-woven to optimize results.

Getting your team to connect your corporate citizen-ship to your company's business strategy has two advan-tages. First, it will help you make your business case for corporate citizenship; second, it will help you to create a plan that really works for the long term, and an agenda that stakeholders will understand and support. The suc-cess you experience as these activities enhance overall business performance will lead to more support. This cre-ates a virtuous cycle that builds upon itself and creates more value for your company and for society.

The context for your corporate citizenship strategy is your company, and your company's context is its market, which exists in the broader context of the global econ-omy, our society, and the planet.

From the Corner Office

To achieve major milestones in corporate citizenship and obtain long-term value, companies must create bold visions and set clear goals. At Dell, those objectives are collected under one ambitious umbrella — their Legacy of Good Plan. Founder and CEO Michael Dell on business and social purpose:

> The changes headed our way require more than incre-mental progress. They demand meaningful change and, for businesses, that starts with a new mindset about corporate responsibility. We have to look beyond our walls to inspire sustainable practices throughout our entire ecosystem, making sustainabil-ity easier for our customers and partners.

That's the 21st goal in our 2020 Legacy of Good Plan, and the one I'm most excited about. We want to develop a methodology for a 360-degree view of our environmental impact.

For example, when we sell a server, we know the carbon footprint for its manufacture and systemic operation. But what if that server is being used to support 100 remote workers who no longer drive to the office? How do we measure that?

We want to understand the totality of our ability to make a positive difference. If we can measure it, we can maximize it. And that's a big opportunity for us all to work together to help ensure our collective future.

Dell Chairman and Chief Executive Officer, **Michael Dell**

From *The Corporate Citizen* magazine, Issue 12, 2015.

WHAT IS STRATEGY?

Strategy today is as much about deciding what not to do as it is about deciding what to do. It's all about making decisions on how to mobilize your resources to get results. Carroll School of Management Dean and innovation expert Andy Boynton teaches his top-rated Boston

College students that in order to be able to mobilize your forces, strategy has to be:

- *Action-oriented*: it describes *what* to do and *why*.

- *Tangible*: it outlines *who* will execute which actions, *the sequence of engagement*, and *how* to measure progress.

- *Important*: it explains *why* you're pursuing one course of action over another, and *what* will be gained and sacrificed.

- *Clear*: it makes your objectives easy to understand. You should be able to explain to a fourth grader *what* is to be done and *why*.

- *Energizing*: your strategy should create a vivid image of success for your team. What does it *look like*? This is a point even great strategists often leave out.

A strategy is an integrated, overarching, clearly communicated concept of how objectives will be achieved. Tactics, on the other hand, comprise a detailed plan of separate actions which are designed to put the strategy into practice.

CONNECTING YOUR CORPORATE CITIZENSHIP TO YOUR BUSINESS STRATEGY

How does your company intend to "win"? For instance, if it has a global growth plan your social investment should help enable that plan, not be entirely domestic. Or if your corporation intends to recruit large numbers of new staff, your programs should focus on how you're going to connect with these new employees. Does the intersection of technology play a major role in your business strategy and if so, how can you leverage that? Or if a large portion of your government business is based on military contracts (e.g., health-care benefit business), you want a sizable presence within the government military sector. Conversely, companies generally should not engage in a cause du jour, e.g., if you have a limited connection to military customers or employees, don't engage in military/veteran programs.

WHICH ASSETS ARE MOST IMPORTANT?

Nobody wants to lose the value they've built in any of their business assets or stakeholder relationships. Remember, however, that strategy is choice and you can't do everything. You'll have to prioritize how you allocate your budgets and what you do first, second, third, and so on.

While we talk about your corporate citizenship strategy, remember your corporate citizenship program is a set of tactics that advances your overall business strategy. So now let's get more specific about how your corporate citizenship can support your business objectives.

Corporate citizenship programs create value for companies in specific ways, and one size doesn't fit all. Take a minute to look at **Table 2**. If you read it from left to right, you can see each resource is most effectively leveraged by different types of programs. This table is useful because it helps to focus on which types of corporate citizenship tactics are best aligned to affect the advantage you are seeking for your company and the change you would like

Table 2: Logic Models for How Corporate Citizenship Creates Business Value

Stakeholder	Effective Activities	Impact on Group	Outcomes	Value to Company	Contingencies
Employees	Sustainability	New skills and training	Eased recruitment and lower turnover	Decreased costs	Industry
	Labor practices	Recruitment and retention	Better teamwork and Higher productivity	Increased revenue	Employee tenure/experience
			Improved performance		
	Philanthropy	Increased engagement			Company size
	Employee volunteering				Perceived authenticity
	Sustainability				
Customers	Cause branding	Higher loyalty	Repurchase and higher share of category spending	Increased market value	Substitutes
	Philanthropy	Favorable reputation	Referrals and willingness to pay premium	Increased revenue	Industry
	Sustainability	Higher satisfaction			Quality of product or service
	Innovation and design	Higher purchase intent			Perception of CSR premium
	Cause marketing				View of authenticity
					Substitutes
Investors	Sustainability	Improved reputation	Lower cost of capital	Decreased costs	Volume of institutional or SRI investors
	Innovation and design	Decreased long-term risk profile	Increased stock valuations	Increased revenue	
	Supply chain management	Expanded product portfolio			
	Disclosure				
	Governance				

	Training programs	Reduce waste	New supplier capability	Reduced cost of production	Scale
Suppliers	Extend ESG standards to suppliers	Lower risk	Share risk across industry where you cannot differentiate	Increase revenue	Competition for resource
	Disclosure requirements	Secure materials and labor predictably	Develop product premium (e.g., fair trade product)	Improved forecast ability	Differentiation of resource
	Codes of conduct/standards	New supplier capability			
Government	Environmental	Develop connections to decision-makers	Reduced lobbying cost	Decreased cost	Maturity of government
	Community involvement	Shape policies and regulatory environment	Access to government purchasing	Increased revenue	Degree of bureaucracy
	Voluntary standards	License to operate			
		Develop consensus standard of operation			
Environment	Pollution reductions	Reduce waste	Alternative materials	Reduced cost of production	Cost of alternatives
	Natural resource conservation	Lower risk	Share risk across industry where you cannot differentiate	Increase revenue	Competition for resource
	Sustainable alternatives	Secure materials predictably	Develop product premium (e.g., fair trade product)	Improved forecast ability	Differentiation of resource
	Codes of conduct/standards	Supply resilience			

to make in the world. When you understand the mechanisms of value creation, you can use your resources more effectively to achieve the results you want.

Because strategy is choice about what you will do and will not do, it is critically important to understand HOW corporate citizenship can create value for your business. When you understand the mechanisms of value creation, you can more effectively deploy resources to yield the results that you seek efficiently.

Connecting Strength to Opportunity

FedEx is admired widely for its logistical and transportation expertise. The company seeks to work with organizations that can benefit from those capabilities. When FedEx executives spoke with the leaders at EMBARQ, the Center for Sustainable Transport at the World Resources Institute, they knew they had found the right fit. EMBARQ works in cities around the globe because 75% of global CO_2 emissions come from cities, and the greatest challenge in addressing that problem is a significant lack of sustainable transportation. FedEx and EMBARQ are now working together on solutions to a problem that will only get worse as urban populations continue to grow. FedEx provides assistance on a number of advisory projects for EMBARQ, including a leadership development program for EMBARQ staff held at FedEx headquarters in Memphis, Tenn. The program helps EMBARQ staff build sustainable public transport and make informed decisions about which buses to purchase for the most fuel-efficient, safe transportation networks. The collaboration between EMBARQ and FedEx is also providing high-quality training to city bus drivers in Mexico City and Guadalajara. Road safety and congestion are significant issues for logistics companies and this partnership not only addresses important social (transportation) and environmental (CO emissions) issues, but also helps to improve the operating context for a company that operates in almost every city in the world.

Reprinted from *The Corporate Citizen* magazine, Summer 2013, Issue 9.

ISSUE FOCUS

Deciding which issues you will try to address with your corporate citizenship program is one of the most important decisions you will make. In addition to thinking about aspects of your business strategy that you can support, there are issues in your operating context that are impacted by your company and that your company can be affected by. These issues can take the form of risks or opportunities.

MAKE SURE YOU'VE COVERED ALL YOUR BASES

Once your team has proposed a corporate citizenship strategy, here are some questions you can use as a lens through which to determine whether the proposal will deliver maximum business and social value.

Does your corporate citizenship strategy fit with your firm's purpose, culture, and corporate strategy?

Do your programs allow everyone at the firm to participate? Who are the leaders of your initiative? Whose patronage do you need to secure for your strategy to be successful? What traditions does your company have that either can be adapted or must be continued? If you introduced the program tomorrow, do you think most employees would think, "Huh?!" or would they have an immediate reaction of, "Of course!"?

Does your corporate citizenship strategy exploit your key resources and capabilities?

For example, Brown-Forman (one of the largest spirit and wine companies in the United States) is a company that uses a lot of water to produce its product and that sources and grows many commodity ingredients such as corn, sugar, and agave. This company would be better suited to focus on soil and water conservation programs than would Microsoft, which would be well suited to working on programs aimed at increasing access to technology (and they each do).

IS YOUR CORPORATE CITIZENSHIP STRATEGY DIFFERENTIATED OR DOES IT HAVE A "ME-TOO" APPROACH?

Most corporate citizenship programs will comprise a portfolio of activities that cover a range of topics and almost all will have some programs that are not differentiated. Think of the federated giving campaigns (United Way) as an example. Unless you are the largest giver, there are few ways for the company to be differentiated, though it is often a community expectation that your company participates. The key in these programs is to derive business value out of the effort by building great employee engagement or learning into your specific process. The ultimate goal is to ensure that most elements of your program are differentiated for your company. There are five criteria to judge this:

1. You adopt, and then improve upon what other companies are doing.

2. The causes you support and the issues you focus on connect logically to your company's core competencies.

3. The causes you support are important to your corporation's employees, community, or customers.

4. You're reinforcing your company's points of difference.

5. You measure the impact of your investments so you can see if you've achieved what you set out to accomplish.

DO YOU HAVE ENOUGH RESOURCES TO PURSUE YOUR STRATEGY?

You may find you have many strategic opportunities with your corporate citizenship program, but you don't have sufficient resources to pursue all (or sometimes any) of them fully. Here's where you have to exercise "generalship" and make decisions about which aspects of your potential strategy are most important to pursue. You can also explore alternative ways to execute your program. Can you deliver an independent signature program, or are there opportunities to reduce costs by working in partnerships? Can you run a smaller pilot program that can be scaled up later?

Can you easily communicate your strategy and describe the value it will deliver (again, and again, and again, and again, etc.)?

You should be able to articulate in a brief statement the value your citizenship program will deliver to your company and society, and why your company is uniquely qualified to deliver that value. It should be simple enough that anyone can understand what you are trying to accomplish. Being repeatable is important, because the average person needs to hear something 3–5 times in order to be able to recall it (never mind act on it).

10 QUESTIONS TO ASK YOUR TEAM BEFORE YOU MOVE ON

1. Can your team define what a strategy is (and what it isn't)?

2. Have we identified key issues of concern to customers, employees, and other stakeholders? In our supply chain?

3. Have we identified issues that are important to our company's success? Have we identified ways our corporate citizenship strategy supports the corporate strategy?

4. What does the future look like if our strategy is successful? How can our corporate citizenship program strengthen our company's strategic position?

5. What will we need to do to get there? Can we engage employees more deeply and address the concerns of investors or customers? Can we create more sustainable and stable supply chains?

6. Have we written our strategy in such a way that all stakeholders can understand it?

7. Do we have the resources to execute our strategy? If not, what choices will we make about what we will do first and what we will not do? What outcomes will be sacrificed as a result?

8. What are the "table stakes" programs that we will have to do because they are expected of everyone?

9. What will our program accomplish for the company that is different than what competitors are doing?

10. How will we measure success? Do we have the resources to measure the impacts we intend?

5

HOW TO SET UP AND ORGANIZE YOUR CORPORATE CITIZENSHIP PROGRAM

THE IMPORTANCE OF NETWORKS AND INFLUENCE

If your corporate citizenship strategy integrates with that of the business, you're three quarters of the way there. Your next step is to organize the team who can advance the environmental and social investments that will differentiate your company.

Your corporate citizenship strategy provides a roadmap for how to identify the people who have a vested interest in achieving corporate citizenship objectives. For example, if disaster relief is a priority you'll need representation from logistics, HR, and communications. Looking to initiate a sustainability report? The person assigned to lead this task will need access to many people in many different operational units. You'll need to ensure that accountability is set to achieve these shared deliverables. Have you identified employee engagement as a citizenship business objective? Then someone in HR should be assigned. Do you think you can reduce your water impact? Connect your environment department, health and safety team, engineering group, and operations leaders to drive that expectation and outcome. Is there a reputation or brand-building opportunity for you? Enlist your communications and marketing team. Effective corporate citizenship will live or die on the accountabilities you set as a senior executive. Optional participation is the most common failure point in every program.

The two diagrams in (**Figure 6**) illustrate the interconnectedness of all areas of your business when it comes to implementing and experiencing your corporate citizenship program. The first uses the example of a disaster relief effort, and the second shows the network you need to build in order to implement measurement and report effectively.

The reason networks are so successful is because each part builds on the strengths of the other; being flexible, they give an organization the stability it requires.

So it's clear when you're working out how to execute your corporate citizenship program that you have to think in a networked way. **Figure 7**, the Galbraith Star Model, provides a simple reminder for executives that if you change one point of your "star model" you need to address all of the rest. This is commonly referred to as "systems thinking." There are five points that link to each other:

- *Strategy*: your plan for competing

- *People*: getting the right group together to do the work

Figure 6: Network Diagram. This figure illustrates different activations of working networks in your company. A single network structure can support two very different activities (sometimes simultaneously). If you have a strong network structure, you have a flexible and resilient team

Activating networks

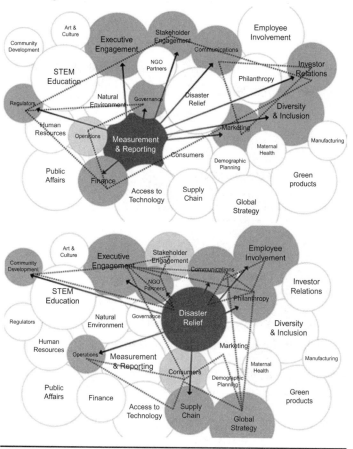

Figure 7: Program Design — Star Model

Source: This figure is reproduced from *Designing Organizations* by Jay R. Galbraith. With permission from Jossey-Bass: San Francisco, 2002.

- *Structure*: organizing the team

- Processes: communicating, making decisions, accomplishing the tasks, measuring progress

- *Metrics and incentives*: keeping people motivated to produce results

If you make changes to one of these areas it has implications for all, so you always have to be thinking about whether you've organized things so you can achieve what you want.

In his book *Designing Dynamic Organizations*,[1] Jay. R. Galbraith created The Star Model™ to visualize how this works. For Galbraith, a strategy is basically a company's formula for success, encompassing the organization's mission as well as its business goals. Its purpose is to create competitive advantage, and to do that a company has to organize the five dimensions of its star to maximize its performance (what it achieves) and its culture (how it achieves). The Galbraith Star Model highlights the multiple dimensions of successful strategy implementation. Galbraith's model reminds us that it is not only about formal structures but also about getting the right people involved, with the right incentives and processes to support the desired outcome. Your teams can develop a Star Model for every program; you have to ensure that you have a comprehensive plan that will yield the performance (what we have achieved) and culture (how you have achieved it) you are seeking.

THE RIGHT STRATEGY

It's important to remember that without the right strategy and accountability your corporate citizenship program is unlikely to succeed short term, and certainly won't be sustainable in the years to come.

THE RIGHT PEOPLE

Getting the right people in your company on board is essential for the success of your strategy implementation. To start this process, here are the roles you should be considering when you're identifying your company's corporate citizenship network:

- The people you want on your teams to do the work.

- Ambassadors for specific campaigns, such as corporate giving or green team initiatives. These people will help you spread the word.

- Project sponsors who have the authority or influence to deploy resources, and who care enough about what you're trying to achieve to use some of their financial or social capital to help you get it done.

Suppose you have a requirement to improve the ethical sourcing in your supply chain. There's bound to be at least one person in your company's procurement department who's ready for a new expanded challenge, and would jump at the chance to be involved in sustainability planning or sourcing more environmentally friendly materials for the company. Giving them the opportunity to interact with their peers on a topic they are interested in, this opportunity provides them with several benefits as well: they broaden their professional network, they get more task variety, and they have the opportunity to demonstrate leadership. In return, you gain an enthusiastic new team member who will need guidance but is also willing to learn.

You'll have realized by now there's a channel which employees always tune into in these situations: it's called What's In It For Me (WIIFM). If you can work out what your opportunity offers them, not only will you engage them more readily but you'll also broaden the net of people you can ask to work with you in the future.

THE RIGHT STRUCTURE

We're moving onto the third point in your system now. How do you create the right structure for your program?

Let's look at an example. When Dave Stangis arrived at Campbell in 2008 he was charged with designing an overarching corporate citizenship strategy, complete with targets and goals in keeping with the values of this nearly 150-year-old company. The plan he developed was organized around four theaters of operation and leveraged a set of cultural norms that existed under previous CEO, Doug Conant, and a lexicon embedded within the culture at that time: environmental stewardship, interactions with customers and consumers, measurable community impact, and building an extraordinary workplace.

Each theater related to a theme built on "nourishing" (the company's mission at the time was Nourishing People's Lives, Everywhere Every Day): the planet, consumers, neighbors, and employees. They were also characterized by an audacious destination goal that was almost impossible to comprehend at the time, but which painted a clear picture of success. The goals were specifically designed to be clear and easy to understand, while also instilling creative tension and demanding change. In 2010, Campbell launched their original 2020 corporate citizenship agenda:

- *Nourishing Our Planet*: reduce the environmental footprint of our product portfolio by half, as measured by water use and CO_2 emissions per product.

- *Nourishing Our Neighbors*: measurably improve the health of young people in our hometown communities by reducing hunger and childhood obesity by 50%.

- *Nourishing Our Employees*: achieve 100% employee engagement in CSR and sustainability.

- *Nourishing Our Consumers*: continue to advance the nutrition and wellness profile of Campbell's product portfolio.

Campbell has continued to evolve with a new strategic framework anchored in its Purpose and its Corporate Citizenship strategy is evolving with it. No matter the point in time, you can see how important getting the necessary buy-in from a diverse range of business units and functions was in making the objective of good corporate citizenship just like any other business objective — one that would advance the company and deliver returns. Remember the purpose of a corporate citizenship strategy isn't simply to do good, but also to drive competitive advantage.

While it was determined from the start that top corporate officers must firmly guide the execution of the strategy, Dave still needed to garner support from wider constituencies across various units and brands. To do this, he used the Star Model we talked about earlier. A pivotal step in the implementation of his strategy at the time was the establishment of governing committees across each theater; he created four executive steering committees that included professionals from across the business units to set and achieve goals. These committees created accountability and fostered the process component: conversation and collaboration enabling Campbell to achieve its corporate citizenship goals. Recognize that your corporate citizenship strategy and any related governance structure will evolve, much like Campbell's has

From the Corner Office

Consider Corporate Citizenship Governance from the Beginning

In my experience at Intel Corporation, later at Campbell Soup Company, and in multiple conversations I have had with my peers and other companies seeking to establish strategic corporate citizenship programs, one key to success comes up time and again — that is to consider and establish a governance structure or structures that drive accountability and enable decision-making. Most companies, of course, have organizations in place to manage human resources, finance, marketing, legal, operations, sales, etc.; however, the corporate citizenship agenda often cuts across many internal organizations and functions and almost always relies on decision-making and accountability outside of traditional organizational structures.

At Intel, I relied upon a management review committee (MRC) convention used at the company for many years. I established a Corporate Responsibility MRC that included key decision-makers and content experts from disciplines such as environmental health and safety, HR, legal, corporate governance, communications, government and public affairs. This group was formally chartered with roles, responsibilities, and oversight functions. It met regularly and intersected with many other formal and matrix organizations across the company. It was critical in driving strategy, enlistment, and results — but perhaps most importantly, being able to weigh company opportunities and make decisions. This was also my sounding board and advisor group. At the time I put it in place, every member was my senior.

At Campbell, I built on those learnings and the Campbell culture to propose to formal governance structures: one at the most senior level of the company in the form of an ultimate steering committee, and the other to oversee and drive the sustainability strategy. These team charters were drafted and shared with the General Counsel and CEO as part of my strategic plan proposal. These concepts were new to these Campbell leaders and they saw great value in the design. They asked me to create three more formally chartered teams that would help guide the workplace, marketplace, and community pillars of the corporate citizenship strategy for Campbell. Each of these teams also had formal governance charters, and were supported and staffed under CEO direction. While I directed the teams, the company's top executives in charge of the various functions were assigned as partners with me. These formally chartered teams, combined with CEO buy-in and support, were critical to jumpstart early action and momentum.

Over time, the governance structures evolved in both companies as corporate citizenship strategies and programs matured. No matter where you are on your corporate citizenship agenda — creating from scratch or taking over a mature program, you have to consider and build into your strategy a governance system to drive accountability and decision-making to fully integrate corporate citizenship into the business operations.

Campbell Soup Company Vice President of Corporate Responsibility, Chief Sustainability Officer, **Dave Stangis**

over Dave's tenure. He is now leveraging an entirely new framework in partnership with CEO Denise Morrison and Campbell's purpose launched in 2014, Real Food that matters for life's moments.

Many companies have created formal as well as informal governance structures around their corporate citizenship programs. Employee councils help provide feedback about the priorities you've set and, by consulting groups of employees in their arenas of influence, will provide feedback about what's working and what's not.

THE RIGHT PROCESSES

Processes cover every element of your corporate citizenship program implementation, including the steps you're taking to recruit people to your team, how they're going to carry out the tasks, how decisions will be made, how you're going to communicate progress, and what methods you'll use to document those processes so others can replicate them.

Here's an example. Suppose you lead a large retail chain that employs many workers who don't have regular access to computers. If you want to recruit a large number of them to participate in your corporate citizenship program, your process would involve going into the stores to talk with managers and associates face to face, or communicating with them via their newsletters or message boards. Whereas in a high-tech company, you would be expected to communicate through digital channels. You use different processes to engage the same number of employees, but it will look different, depending on the environment.

Communication processes are obviously critical, but there are also execution processes. Take, for example, the green teams we discussed earlier. If you have ambassadors from all over your company who have offered to be part of your initiative, not all of them will be capable of executing your plan without support. Let's face it, many have probably never done anything like this before. So you'll need to provide them with step-by-step directions for what you want them to do, and support them while they execute it. One of the processes Campbell has implemented to deepen employee involvement in their corporate citizenship program is to create an orientation module for new employees as part of their regular onboarding. It begins by explaining what sustainability and corporate citizenship mean at Campbell, then goes on to provide information about how employees can become involved in the program and learn more. It has proven to be a simple, low-cost way to make everyone aware of the corporate citizenship mission and opportunities. Without this orientation, many people would spend months or even years wondering how to connect with them, whereas now they know what to do from day one. Dave has a small team at Campbell, and the team can tell you one of his mantras is converting people passion to business process. It is the way to make corporate citizenship "stick."

You'll also need to decide where the lines of responsibility are drawn between your committees and yourself. Are you going to have meetings, and if so how often? Who is going to do what? Are they providing input, or are they decision-makers? Remember to document it so your team knows what to expect and how to communicate progress.

THE RIGHT METRICS AND INCENTIVES

The people you've organized to implement your processes are more likely to stay engaged with your initiative if it's clear to them how you will measure and reward success. Establishing agreed upon metrics is vital in that they communicate progress, so everyone can understand what's been achieved.

Different employee groups are motivated by different things. If early career employees who are very interested in developing professional networks are praised publicly for contributions to corporate citizenship projects and, as a result, their efforts catch the attention of top level executives, this group may perceive executive attention as more beneficial even than praise from direct supervisors. For more experienced executives, the reward is more likely to come from getting involved with something bigger than him or herself, which leaves the world (and the company) in a better place. It is an expression of a personal legacy.

Consider all your levers of motivation and incentives including pay incentives. Among managers and executives, compensation is a growing part of the reward structure.[2]

METRICS AND MEASUREMENT

It's worth taking a moment here to focus on how you're going to measure the results of your program.

The questions to ask yourself are: what would you *like* to measure, and what can you *actually* measure?

Depending on your company's current capabilities and resources, you may not be able to measure all outcomes or even impacts.

Start internally. What are the key performance metrics of your strategy based on the what we've covered so far in this book? Will you be seeking to assess your company's energy use, greenhouse gas emissions, waste generation and recycling, and water use? How about employee volunteer hours, training and development, and investments? Would you include product and service-related items, such as packaging improvements, sales from improved product lines, and consumer or stakeholder perceptions? Getting to the Key Performance Indicators (KPIs) and baseline data for your company can be a major undertaking, so don't underestimate the time your team will need. You'll create a better program if you decide the metrics and measures during the design phase. Begin with the end in mind.

THE ONLY CONSTANT IS CHANGE

Finally, remember one of the constants in business is change. A common reason why corporations seek our help at the Boston College Center for Corporate Citizenship is because there's been a change of top management and priorities are shifting. An alteration in strategy means you may need to adjust your whole organizational ecosystem for success (your star design) to address changes in personnel, strategy, or work processes. This can be unsettling for the team that has been pulled together to execute your company's corporate citizenship strategy. It may be a time when you pull back and focus on those elements of your program that are less aspirational and more focused on enhancing persistent operational goals, like keeping employees engaged or finding operational efficiencies. Every shift in organization or strategy can be a moment of opportunity.

10 QUESTIONS TO ASK YOUR TEAM BEFORE YOU MOVE ON

1. Have we drawn a map of our network — the people who can help implement our plans?

2. Have we identified who will serve as workers, ambassadors, and sponsors? Do we have a healthy number of each, and in the right places? What can we do to get a critical mass in key departments?

3. Have we worked out an influencing strategy for approaching and motivating the people in these new areas?

4. Can we describe our corporate citizenship structure? Have we created an organization that allows for feedback and decision-making from key contributors?

5. Do people understand their roles and the accountability they have to the project and each other?

6. Can we describe the WIIFM for each member of our corporate citizenship network?

7. What processes do we currently use, and how could they be improved? Are they documented? Does everyone understand how they should be implemented?

8. What metrics can we measure today? What metrics do we believe we need to measure that we can't measure today?

9. How will we communicate these metrics and measurements to our team?

10. Have we defined a set of incentives that we want to use or create? Which are in place now and which are part of our future plans?

NOTES

1. Galbraith, Downey, and Kates (2001).
2. Boston College Center for Corporate Citizenship (2015).

SECTION 2

GETTING RESULTS ACROSS YOUR BUSINESS

6

THE IMPORTANCE OF YOUR SUPPLY CHAIN AND PROCUREMENT FUNCTION

The procurement and supply chain processes are the richest and fastest growing area for most companies to identify risks and opportunities for corporate citizenship programs. Your supply chain can hold big challenges for a company's corporate citizenship performance and reputation, yet can also provide the most significant opportunities to address them.

Why is corporate citizenship so integral to procurement? Because for every material or service your company buys, there are issues to monitor and manage, from a risk and opportunity perspective. If you don't invest time in understanding your supply chain, there's an activist or advocate group that will be monitoring it for you. From human rights to climate change, from biodiversity to animal welfare, and from toxic substances to diversity in employment, there's a huge range of issues to contend with. Ethical supply chain management has also gone from being a reactive business discipline to a very much proactive one — it has to be. Ten years ago, if something went wrong in your supply chain, your company would have days or even weeks to investigate and fix it. Today with the explosion of social media, you'll be lucky to have an hour. And you will probably not even be the first to know about it.

So get it right and you can create a competitive advantage. Get it wrong and the consequences can be enormous.

By the way, this will never be perfect; your supply chain is too complex for that, and issues change over time. Categorizing your risks is simply a way of helping you prioritize where to focus first, narrowing down that overwhelming complexity.

The next step is identifying groups of suppliers (or your inputs) by risk level. Group them into low, medium, and high-risk companies or materials. This will be of great help when you set priorities for the next few steps.

You can think about the risk inherent in your supply chain in a few different ways:

- Size of risk

- Reputation impacts of the topic or area of risk to your customers or the community

- Long-standing practices known to be risky or less transparent

- Suppliers your company spends the most money with — is a large proportion of your spend with a few suppliers?

Choice of suppliers — do you trade with companies that are the sole source of supply for a particular product? Are they working in a geographic region where there are geopolitical or environmental risks inherent?

WORKING WITH CODES AND STANDARDS OF CONDUCT

There are many codes of conduct that set rules to define what's ethical and responsible, and what's not. This means someone else has done work assessing and prioritizing risks in any given area, which can only be of help to your company. Understanding these helps creates an ethical supply chain approach in your business.

If your corporation is similar to most, your team will need to work with preexisting codes of conduct that outline the standards of behavior expected of your company and its procurement team. There are probably at least 50 different examples of third-party codes of conduct you should be aware of, and we'll be giving you some examples in this section.

Codes of conduct are basically rules set up for how you conduct business and manage your suppliers (including how your suppliers manage their suppliers). You can see they're integral to help you manage risks in this area, although they're also very complex.

You may have had the foresight to assign one person to manage all of the codes of conduct for your company, but it's more likely that there are many codes located around the business and they have to be identified and summarized. Once you've had your team do that you can start to catalog all the codes of conduct your company needs to abide by, either because you've written them yourself, or because third parties have set them for you, based on the sector you operate in.

This list can get long. For instance, many suppliers around the world work toward similar expectations in relation to human rights. Given that the United Nations and the International Labor Organization have standards for protecting and establishing human rights standards, it doesn't matter what business you're in — recognizing and having systems around the protection of these rights is universal.

It gets more specific in the environmental arena. The expectations here can be wide-ranging, going beyond compliance with local laws or even international conventions. There is a significant number of benchmarks set externally for the kind of business you're in. For example, in the food sector Oxfam is well known for their review of the supply chain focusing on transparency, women and children in the workforce, how people are treated on farms, the difference between small and large farmers, how land is managed, biodiversity, fertilizer use, and more.[1] Advocacy groups like this do the research in the field and try to hold companies accountable, moving the needle a bit every year so companies like yours are continually encouraged to improve.

There are a couple of interesting examples in the electronics sector as well. One that focuses on technology products is Electronic Product Environmental Assessment Tool (EPEAT, http://www.epeat.net/), which is a standard for how green a company's electronic products are. It takes into account how the components are made, how energy efficient they are, and where they come from. So any purchasing body, including the US government, can use a standard like EPEAT to help decide whether they're going to require electronics purchases from a manufacturer that adheres to these guidelines.

You can see how these global bodies can set expectations of behavior around the world. When companies want to show they respect human rights, for instance, they will often say they act in accordance with the UN Global Compact or the ILO Conventions.

In addition to external organizations (such as nonprofits and the United Nations) creating codes of conduct, companies within the same sector are increasingly banding together to create their own. One of the first was the Electronics Industry Code of Conduct (developed by the Electronics Industry Citizenship Coalition (EICC), http://www.eiccoalition.org/). This was created by global brands such as Intel, Microsoft, and Motorola coming together to work with activists and NGOs in order to create a uniform set of expectations for human rights and environmental performance across the supply chain. They realized that, big as they were, the problem was too large for each of them to track and manage on their own. Now there are similar frameworks in place across the consumer goods world, including The Consumer Goods Forum, which is made up of hundreds of food and consumer goods manufacturers and retailers such as Unilever, Nestle, Danone, Campbell, and Procter & Gamble along with retailers such as Walmart, Marks & Spencer, Kroger, and Walgreens/Boots.[2]

From the Corner Office

ArcelorMittal recognizes the power that clear corporate citizenship goals can have on engaging with stakeholders and meeting business objectives. As a global leader in steel production, ArcelorMittal is also a leader in sustainable operations with a commitment to a long-term strategy.

> Corporate citizenship issues have a direct impact on businesses, as well as individuals, governments, and civil society. We are expected to be part of the solution and bring value to society more broadly through our products, the way we operate, and our core purpose.

> While we have made good progress on our sustainability agenda over the eight years since the creation of ArcelorMittal, that agenda continues to evolve. We must respond to evolving social and environmental trends, which is why we've created 10 sustainable development outcomes we plan on delivering over the long term. We know that being able to adapt is crucial in all aspects of our business.

> Sustainability has to be a priority because ultimately it is about building a better and stronger future for ArcelorMittal. Whether it is the importance of our people's safety or the value we bring — not only from our products — but also the social and economic value from our production sites, or being trusted by our communities and our customers for the way we use natural capital. All of this is crucial if we want to enjoy the support of our stakeholders.

Arcelor Mittal Chairman and Chief Executive Officer, **Lakshmi N. Mittal**

From *The Corporate Citizen* magazine, Issue 12, 2015.

INTEGRATING YOUR CORPORATE CITIZENSHIP STRATEGY WITH YOUR PROCUREMENT TEAM'S WORK

As you realize by now, a central theme of this book is the importance of embedding your corporate citizenship work into your company's existing objectives. Now you know the risks and opportunities present in your supply chain, and you have an understanding of the relevant codes of conduct. Next, your team will need to work to integrate this knowledge into your corporate citizenship strategy. The process is similar to what you did with your stakeholders; your projects need to have supply chain requirements imprinted upon them. This will help your company develop more resilient systems to manage the risks inherent in your supply chain and allow you to take advantage of inherent opportunities as well.

You also need to decide whether you will ask your suppliers to sign your company's code of conduct and whether you will also conduct regular inspections. If this is the case, would you do the visit, or would you send a third-party inspector? Bear in mind, there's a window of risk for whatever you do. So for your high-risk suppliers, for instance, you might visit once a year whereas for your middle-risk suppliers it would be every other year. Your low-risk suppliers might just be expected to sign an affirmation of compliance. These are just examples for how you can adjust oversight and management based on risk, tolerance, and resilience.

The most important part is not how you manage codes of conduct but how you set expectations, how you communicate them, and how you decide on the process to manage risk. Who owns and is accountable for that?

MOVING FROM RISK TO REWARD

When you first start to examine your supply chain, everything is going to look like risk; and, people being what we are, we're more afraid of risk than we are motivated toward reward. Your main opportunity is to move from being reactive to proactive, to help your company anticipate and prepare, and to find areas in which your company can differentiate itself from its competitors in a positive way. What do you want to be known for — not having anything 'bad' going on, or for actually driving the agenda for change? You can see this particularly well in companies that source a single core ingredient such as cocoa, paper, or coffee. Because they rely so heavily on one kind of material, many of them have stepped up to help farmers create a more sustainable process for growing that also works economically for their customers, for example using fair trade or responsibly sourced ingredients.

This is the way you move away from being reactive or defensive — "We're on TV for ——————————" (fill in the blank here with any negative event that worries you) to becoming positively proactive and talking about the improvements you've made. One method of doing this is to assess and score your suppliers for their performance and even to build a recognition program for your highest performing suppliers, which can motivate all to aspire to be the best.

PEOPLE ARE AT THE HEART OF YOUR SUPPLY CHAIN

Once you start looking at your supply chain from both an internal and external perspective, how do you train the people who manage it? How do you help your own company get smarter with its systems, so underlying issues don't develop into crises?

Corporate citizenship within your supply chain isn't just about standards and monitoring, but about making your company more effective. And you do this through communicating expectations to your suppliers via your procurement team.

This is a business opportunity, not a tax on the system. Find ways to help your buyers go from being people who only negotiate for the best price to pioneers who find opportunities in all their sourced materials and services.

Earlier we touched on creating a recognition system for your suppliers. This creates a win–win situation and can also reflect well on the buyer involved. By doing this, you're building a way forward for your suppliers to share where they're doing ethical work, helping your team learn more over time. Your suppliers will appreciate the recognition among their own customers for building a sustainable, responsible, and resilient supply chain because it's an important selling tool for them. A tiered approach, in which you recognize the best and encourage the others to aspire to match them, encourages your suppliers to compete around human rights, ethical servicing, and responsible sourcing, thereby helping you to manage your strategy and reduce risk.

Your main task, in mapping out your supply chain risks and opportunities, is to think about the social, human, and environmental aspects of how you source your products and services. It's an incredibly rich and diverse area.

10 QUESTIONS TO ASK YOUR TEAM BEFORE YOU MOVE ON

1. Have we mapped out our suppliers and vendors through a formal process, assigning risks and opportunities?

2. Have we identified the key risk areas for both our business and our sector?

3. Have we decided how far down in our supply chain system you will go, or will we deal with first tier suppliers only?

4. Do we have a written code of conduct or set of supplier expectations that's easily available to our suppliers (actual and potential)?

5. Does our supplier code of conduct include expectations in the social (human rights, labor, community) and environmental (legal compliance, resource management, energy efficiency) dimensions?

6. What process have we identified for evolving our supply chain issues within our business and sector?

7. Have we defined ownership and accountability for ethical supply chain performance?

8. Have we identified and implemented a communications process to ensure our suppliers (actual and potential) understand and uphold our expectations?

9. Have we communicated and implemented an action program to deal with problem suppliers?

10. Have we established any capacity building components in our supply chain strategy, such as ongoing training or joint strategy development with key suppliers?

NOTES

1. https://www.oxfamamerica.org/explore/research-publications/impact-updates/. Accessed on April 9, 2017.

2. For a full list, visit http://www.theconsumergoodsforum.com/about-the-forum/our-members

7

CREATING A MORE SUSTAINABLE OPERATION

In this chapter, it's time to turn your attention inward to your own company and how sustainably it runs its own operations. In Chapters 6 and 7, you'll notice we're taking a business flow (or value chain) approach — from the supply chain to the internal business as we discuss corporate citizenship. This order isn't set in stone. It may make more sense to you to focus on your internal operations before you address your supply chain. There's no wisdom in the particular order you dig into these areas, just that you think about them both in a strategic way. There are multiple opportunities waiting for you here — you just need to do a bit of digging to find them. In this chapter you'll learn how to choose the most productive areas to focus on, so that you can make your business a model for your suppliers and competitors to follow.

Why should you go to this effort? Because it's the right thing to do of course, but that's not actually the main reason. The big incentive for you to take a magnifying glass to your own company is that there's a direct

From the Corner Office

As a company that has been growing for more than a century, Kimberly-Clark knows about sustainable and socially responsible progress.

At Kimberly-Clark, we make our vision to lead the world in essentials for a better life a reality by building a sustainable enterprise. We strive to innovate with proper regard for our environment. That is why we set five-year stretch goals to reduce our environmental impact and increase the positive impact on our communities.

We continuously ask: How do we go landfill free in all of our manufacturing? How can we consume less water in our processes? How can we create an equivalent amount of water in the communities where we operate that will provide for people in water-stressed areas? How do we reduce the total amount of greenhouse gases from our production? Then, we set aggressive goals for every one of our operations around the world, and we track our progress.

Behaving this way keeps us true to the values that Kimberly-Clark was built on. One hundred forty years ago, our founders believed in three things — manufacturing quality products, providing great service, and dealing fairly with our employees and communities. And we still believe in that today.

Kimberly-Clark Corporation Chairman and Chief Executive Officer, **Thomas J. Falk**

From *The Corporate Citizen* magazine, Issue 12, 2015.

alignment between making it more sustainable and making it more efficient, profitable, and innovative. You have a golden opportunity to bring value to the bottom line, build competitive advantage in your marketplace, and develop your team's business acumen in the process.

SETTING YOUR BASELINE METRICS

Before you start trying to improve your company's environmental efficiency, you need to find out how it's performing right now. How much energy and water does your enterprise use today? How much waste does it generate? How are your corporation's internal functions performing in the environmental realm as we speak?

Let's start with the big three: energy, water, and waste. You can't create a sustainability strategy without getting good baseline data on these, at a minimum. Once you have set up a measurement system to track these data, you'll start finding opportunities everywhere you look. Think of your data as being the fuel that feeds the forward motion; as you know what to measure and how to drive accountability for the results of your strategy, others see the value, which in turn provides more leverage in the business. Just be sure to give credit where it's due — to the teams driving and investing in the work.

You and your teams will probably find delving into energy, water, and waste to be a challenge, but it's also an amazing exercise to help you understand more about your company's major environmental footprint today. We'll take each of these three areas in turn below.

ENERGY

Energy feeds everything in your business, and with climate change and renewable energy getting so much attention there are many opportunities to make sustainable changes. The term "energy" can cover elements including electricity, natural gas, fuels, and even steam. What's more, your company's energy use isn't only related to what it needs to run its base operations, but also covers the energy used by your suppliers as well as that related to the transportation of products and employees.

So how do you find out how much energy your company uses in its operations? Some companies may have this information available already (although not necessarily all in one place), and if yours does that's great, but even then you need to understand the context and what the numbers mean.

There are resources for this. If you are operating in the United States, the Environmental Protection Agency (EPA) has tools to help translate the information you find internally into greenhouse gas equivalents.[1] You can also check out the greenhouse gas protocol developed by the World Resources Institute[2] and the information on energy published by the World Business Council for Sustainable Development.[3]

Your task at this stage is simply to figure out what you do and don't know. Don't get bogged down in the complexity of it all — you'll never discover everything to do with your company's energy use. Just establish some principles and baseline measures which you can use. Ask yourself how well you can answer this question: how much energy does my company use, and where does it use?

Making Carbon Neutral Cost-Effective

In 2012, Microsoft established an internal "carbon fee." It began charging its own business divisions for their carbon emissions based on their energy consumption including electricity use and business air travel. This dramatic move helped the company achieve its goal of carbon neutrality and net-zero emissions for its data centers, software development labs, offices, and other functions. "We instituted a carbon fee last year because it had the potential to ignite a culture change, and that's exactly what's starting to happen," says Rob Bernard, Microsoft's chief environmental strategist. "A carbon price means that we now have a common language for how to drive awareness around and begin to reduce emissions. It's made environmental sustainability an increasingly important part of how Microsoft does business." The carbon fee has helped support both energy savings projects at Microsoft and increased purchases of renewable power to make Microsoft the second largest purchaser of green power in the United States, according to the U.S. Environmental Protection Agency. The carbon fee also helped fund a new power purchase agreement Microsoft made to buy the energy from a new 100 MW wind farm in Texas.

First published in *The Corporate Citizen* magazine, Winter 2014, Issue 10.

WATER

Water is usually a simpler area to measure than energy. If your business isn't large, it might be as easy as pulling out your last few water bills. However, most big corporations derive their water from more than just one source; they might get it from surface water (rivers, lakes, or streams), wells, recycled water systems, and gray water sources. Almost every major manufacturer on the planet has a significant need for water in every aspect of their production process.

Not only do you need to understand how *much* water you use, but also where it comes from, *how* it's used, and where it goes once you've finished with it — how much goes into making your products, and how much gets recycled or pumped back into the original or alternate sources or into municipal treatment systems.

WASTE

Waste is usually the easiest area to get baseline data on. Your business will almost certainly have a contract with a waste vendor or recycling facility, so it shouldn't be too difficult to measure how much waste is leaving the building, how much is being recycled, how much is going into landfill, and how much is going to a hazardous waste treatment facility.

Depending on what kind of business you operate, you might find there are more waste measures which are specific to your company or sector. For example, some manufacturers emit waste into the air. These substances go by different acronyms which may be important for you to understand, for instance, volatile organic compounds (VOC), and oxides of nitrogen (NO_x) and sulfur (SO_x). Particulates and ozone are key air pollutants and are the main precursors of smog around the world. Understanding these details can get a little challenging when you're not a manufacturing expert, but just get your head around the top line information.

The great thing is that what kinds of waste your company is generating, and how it deals with it are key measures to work out which go straight to the financial bottom line. No business is in place to manufacture waste, so when you identify ways to reduce it that's a double win for your company and your community.

BRINGING YOUR METRICS TOGETHER

No matter what type of company you work for, you could potentially measure tens if not hundreds of inputs and outputs to do with energy, water, and waste. This would be a full-time job and is of course totally impractical.

Instead, figure out the two to five major areas that are most relevant for your business. For example, if you're a timber company producing wood, paper, pulp, and corrugate, you might create a separate set of data for each output. One of your key business indicators would be the number of products you can make from a certain number of trees, and your objective would be to increase the volume of output for the resources you use.

HOW TO TURN YOUR BASELINE DATA INTO GOALS AND TARGETS

So now that you have baseline measures in place it's time to take action. How will you create goals and performance targets, based on the starting points you've identified?

First, do some easy benchmarking. Look to your peers and competitors if you need a quick level set on the key metrics for your own business. As a minimum, you want to be able to assess and communicate the same types of environmental data your competitors use (and ideally you want to do better). All businesses live to compete, so challenge your management team on what your competition is doing on KPIs. Even businesses outside your sector can be motivational because they demonstrate what's possible.

CONTEXT-BASED GOALS

Before you go any further into goal setting, it's helpful to understand new ways of thinking called "context-based," or sometimes "science-based," goals. Leading companies are evolving their reasoning around environmental goal setting, so instead of stating that they're going to reduce their water use by 3% next year, they look at whether or not that makes sense in their business and geography. A corporation with a manufacturing facility based in the Arizona desert might create a more aggressive water reduction strategy than one operating out of Seattle or London, for instance.

This makes a lot of sense, from both a business and risk perspective. You may have read about the global environmental standards produced by agreements such as the

Kyoto Protocol, COP21, or the Paris Accord. These aren't focused on a single company reducing energy use by 2%, rather they demand a reduction of greenhouse gases globally. More and more companies are looking at their goals and attaching them to this global context, rather than simply looking inward to their own performance.

This is much harder to envision than a simple, internal corporate goal. Everybody understands what a 1% or 2% reduction means, but signing up for some impact in society that's different in one place compared to another can be much more challenging. It might lead you to avoid sourcing ingredients from areas that are water scarce, for example. So although it makes sense to think about goals in this way because you're looking at the bigger picture, it's a lot harder to communicate in a language that's understandable to most executives. After all, they didn't go into business to worry about how their company will keep the climate from increasing in temperature by more than two degrees centigrade, did they? How would you measure the effect your efforts are having on the world? And how much could you claim "credit" for, if you're a food company compared to an automotive manufacturer?

This is an emerging area, but over the next few years it's going to become a growing part of the reputation narrative so it's a good idea to become familiar with it now.

EMPLOYEE HEALTH AND WELL-BEING

Increasingly, potential employees make decisions about where they want to work based on how safe they think their workplace will be, the benefits they will receive, and how good they perceive the culture to be in terms of taking care of their physical and emotional health. Employee health and well-being is a key opportunity area for companies in the 21st century.

If you feel your company could do more to make itself attractive to employees (and which company couldn't?), this isn't something that happens on its own: you need to help drive the agenda. Potential employees have heard about the cool workplaces being developed in the tech world, which is creating a trickle-down set of expectations for all employees. Nowadays many businesses have fitness centers, in-house nutritionists, relaxing break areas, on-site childcare, parental leave, and other amenities, in order to create an environment in which employees enjoy working and feel safe.

How would you create baseline measures for these benefits or the amount of money your corporation invests in employee well-being, and how would you track it going forward?

Of course you don't need to become an expert in health and safety, but you do need to help your company set targets and report progress.

BUILDINGS AND FACILITIES

Believe it or not, your physical place of work is often the most effective place to start bringing corporate citizenship to life. If you think about it, putting a dedicated effort into improving the sustainability of your workplace not only pays cost-saving dividends, but can also play a key role in strengthening your company culture around your commitment to being environmentally friendly. Whether you operate in a single building, a leased space, a network of buildings, or in a huge corporation, you can increase your sustainability in many different ways.

How do you go about this? Several resources exist to help make your workplace greener. These range from user-friendly technology to formal research. For information about building standards, take a look at the U.S. Green Building Council's LEED standards[4]; these focus on improving design and sustainability in the building itself. For technology, there are smart systems you can investigate: sensors that turn lights on and off depending on whether people are around, temperature systems that know when people are in the building, and water-use devices that take gray water and recycle it, to name but a few. Even low-tech initiatives such as having different bins for recycling and regular waste are a step forward.

In terms of your actual offices, there are all kinds of opportunities for improving sustainability in furnishing and furniture, building materials, seating, desks, and technology. Each one of these has a sustainability story behind it. Remember, your company's employees are its best ambassadors, so if you want it to have an environmentally friendly image on the outside, you need to reflect that from the inside by walking the talk.

You have multiple chances to create an internal culture of sustainability through the use of company signage and notices. Actually, it's often employees themselves who have the best ideas about how to make their workplace more environmentally friendly. You could crowd-source suggestions from them. This could be as simple as having a suggestion box, or as technical as creating an online platform which allows people to rate ideas. Experience shows that an effective way to achieve improvement is to give employees accountability for implementing their own suggestions; if they have the assignment to figure out what they want in a cost-effective way, they'll own the idea as well as need to sell it, which means they'll feel motivated to make it come to life.

TRAVEL AND TRANSPORTATION

Unlike buildings, travel isn't something you can "see" which is why most people overlook it. However, it's actually a part of your workplace facilities and impact.

Take commuting for instance — there are many things you can do to promote greener options. This could range from company parking spaces dedicated to shared pool cars, to providing incentives for people to bike to work. Charging stations for electric cars have become expected, and many electric utilities will install these for zero or low cost. When you multiply the incremental environmental benefits for one employee by thousands, you can see how this can be an area of high impact.

You can also build recognition systems for community involvement around sustainability. Almost every local municipality in the developed world has some kind of local partnership in which they're working with companies to share best practices — yours is bound to have one. Consider other local businesses, or merchants where your employees may shop, as potential partners for your employee focused programs. For instance, a local car retailer could offer your employees discounts on electric or hybrid cars, or the local utility may have discounts on roof-mounted solar panels. Don't forget to find a way to highlight employees who take advantage of these benefits.

Stepping back from individuals, let's look at business travel and fleet management. Most travel agents have efficiency programs you can implement. Each time they book a flight for an employee and they can show the greenhouse gas impact of it in the itinerary; at that point either the employee or their company can choose to offset the impact by paying a small premium, or planting trees, or some other parallel offset activity. At the end of the year, the agent can report how many miles your company has flown and even what the CO_2 emissions were. It's a great piece of information to communicate the fact you're monitoring it, and also to prove you're making positive changes.

Even rental car operators can help you identify greener options in your company fleet; there's a lot of innovation out there to help you, and it's usually free — just ask. Courier contracts are another place to look for improvements. The big firms have amazing programs that can help you build sustainable practices that save costs and energy, such as grouping collections into certain days of the week. Even large office supply companies have environmental sustainability strategies to help corporations, and they're just waiting for your call. On the broader logistical front, there are many other tools. For instance, there's an external framework for the U.S. EPA called SmartWay, which is a certification for road trucks covering a range of areas from fuel efficiency to aerodynamics; you can ask your suppliers to ensure their trucks are SmartWay certified.[5]

So you can see how much free help is out there for your teams to access. The beauty of it is that it's incredibly measurable and cost efficient, a win—win for both you and your corporation.

SUSTAINABLE PACKAGING

If you work for a consumer goods company, or any business manufacturing a physical product, the packaging you use is a key opportunity for environmental advantage.

Like all the changes we've talked about in this chapter, packaging doesn't become sustainable on its own; your company needs an overt strategy, and it's not an easy area. Although there are cost benefits for companies in, for instance, making their packaging lighter in weight, the consumer is looking for convenience. Consumers have grown to love individually packaged products especially when they're shipped from online retailers; everything comes in its own little box with its own bubble wrap. So unlike transportation or even energy, where moving to a more sustainable system is always win—win, packaging can be more challenging to improve. That's why you need to be very deliberate in how you tackle it.

The key to this is leveraging packaging suppliers and vendors. Agree to a set of goals and ask them to incorporate, for example, recycled materials wherever possible. Another option is to reduce secondary packaging (that's packaging which goes around the original to keep the product safe during shipping or distribution) or to send the packaging back to your supplier for recycling once you've received the goods. There are many ideas you can implement, and it can be a good opportunity for innovation. Just don't forget to track key metrics and measure your progress. You don't want to eliminate a million pounds of packaging and miss the chance to communicate your environmental and bottom line savings.

One way to make this simpler but also to unlock tremendous value is to create objectives during packaging redesign or at critical packaging decision points. This means every time a product is being reviewed and its packaging redesigned, someone takes the time to determine if it can be made lighter in weight, more renewable, or recyclable. Just asking these questions can go a long way toward transforming your business's packaging footprint. They won't get asked on their own. You need baseline measures, a strategy, and longer-term goals in place before product managers implement a new design.

Although consumers value convenience, they also love the message recycled and recyclable packaging sends to them; it's a clear indicator the company is serious about sustainability. As a result, it's one of the most straightforward ways to send a credible environmental message without spending money on advertising. You're demonstrating to consumers on an individual basis; you're not just *saying* the right things, you're actually *doing* them. One of the most notable examples of this happened when Dell began developing packaging from 100% compostable mushrooms and straw. The package was so benign to the environment, it was literally edible. Company founder Michael Dell demonstrated it as such when he ate a bit of it dipped in soy sauce in front of a sustainable business audience in 2015.[6]

THE CYCLE OF INNOVATION

You are aware by now that tackling your company's internal environmental footprint is an innovative process, where teams work alongside diverse external and internal functions to change processes that may have been in place for decades. Tapping into the innovation cycle is absolutely critical if you want this work to embed itself in the overall innovation process.

For instance, why does your company use one transportation or packaging supplier instead of another which offers more environmentally friendly products or services? If you know when and where this kind of decision is made, who makes it, and how it's measured, you're able to instill a process that can deliver a larger and longer lasting impact.

In time, you can go from simply reducing energy and water use to driving what gets funded for a capital project and even the characteristics of companies considered for mergers and acquisitions. For instance, when a new building is being planned, employee well-being and sustainable design criteria can be considered as part of the process, rather than an afterthought.

If you put these leadership and management strategies in place within your corporate citizenship strategy, you'll start to create real value and position your company for the next century, while building competitive advantage for your company. It's a long-term effort and one of the toughest areas of corporate citizenship, but it's essential. It's an achievement that will remain in place long after you've retired.

10 QUESTIONS TO ASK YOUR TEAM BEFORE YOU MOVE ON

1. Have we defined the resource footprints of our enterprise (energy, water and waste use, waste generation, and emissions)?

2. Have we determined baseline measurements for our enterprise for those key resource footprints?

3. If we're a major player in our sector, do we understand the concept of context-based or science-based goal setting?

4. Do we have clear expectations that our workplace should be safe and healthy, and supporting practices and measures that are clearly communicated?

5. Have we employed practices and technologies in our workplace to drive energy and resource reductions, as well as to build a culture around sustainability? For example, have we evaluated our travel and transportation activities from both an employee and supply chain perspective?

6. Do our employees have a clear way to provide input to our workplace corporate citizenship strategies, and to celebrate their successes?

7. Have we evaluated our packaging footprint from both a purchasing and marketplace perspective? Do we know our baseline? Have we identified opportunities to drive a more sustainable packaging footprint?

8. Can we describe our key processes and where we can improve workforce development, material procurement, business operations, product development, and delivery?

9. Have we incorporated simple, comprehensive corporate citizenship and sustainability considerations into these business decision processes?

10. Have we established accountability and governance for enterprise-wide decisions relative to sustainability?

NOTES

1. https://www.epa.gov/research/methods-models-tools-and-databases

2. http://www.ghgprotocol.org/standards/corporate-standard

3. http://www.wbcsd.org/publications-and-tools.aspx

4. http://www.usgbc.org/leed. Accessed on April 9, 2017.

5. https://www.epa.gov/smartway/learn-about-smartway. Accessed on April 9, 2017.

6. https://www.crn.com.au/news/michael-dell-eats-mushroom-pc-packaging-386147. Accessed on April 9, 2017.

8

DEFINING YOUR CORPORATE GIVING PROGRAM

There are many ways to describe corporate giving: shared value, impact-investing, collective impact, strategic philanthropy — just to name a few. As we are writing this book, there are probably five new terms being developed to describe the practice. Don't worry about what you call your program.

Corporate gifts managed in a strategic way add value to society and improve your company's operating context. The most effective corporate giving programs invest in causes and issues that are important to the company's community, employees, customers, and others in your sphere of operation. Developing corporate giving and employee involvement programs that address issues important to these key stakeholders and arenas is an effective way to create value for the business and the community.

There should be an obvious, logical connection between your corporate giving strategy and your business strategy — one that's obvious to all your stakeholders — and not only to those who actively engage in your program.

Your stakeholders should be able to discern why you're investing in one particular purpose and not another. If you can do this, you've reached a strategic "sweet spot." What's more, if there's a strategic fit, you'll be able to describe your giving program in a clear and understandable way whether you're communicating to a local nonprofit or your board of directors. What are you trying to accomplish? For whom and through whom?

WHEN IS SMALL BIG?

For most companies, there's a combined need to support causes that connect to business strategy, *and* to invest in charities that are dear to employees' hearts, or that address critical needs in the communities where they operate, but which are otherwise unrelated to the business.

Sometimes these more distributed approaches can do good in ways that are incidental to the original purpose of the gifts. An example of this is companies that build recognition programs to encourage employee engagement with giving campaigns. The company can create value from this distributed approach by celebrating employee participation and leadership. Employee recognition is a crucial ingredient to deriving business value from many small, unfocused gifts.

From the Corner Office

Toyota Financial Services is led by the belief that embracing differences is key to both business and corporate citizenship goals, the company holds diversity and inclusion at the forefront of its efforts to create both a positive workplace culture and a strong bottom line.

At Toyota Financial Services, we know our success relies on our people, and in this our position is very simple — we must include and engage as many types of people as possible. The key to our future is about embracing our differences and not defending our similarities. The more we do that, the better organization we're going to be.

Diversity and inclusion is a major component of our corporate citizenship program, and of the way we run our business in general. We realized a few years ago that when you're working with people that have the same backgrounds, the same characteristics, the same experiences, then the outcome becomes pretty predictable. We embarked on a training program to make sure that we weren't treating diversity and inclusion as a marketing campaign — but instead as a sustainable culture change.

For us, it's more than just a nice thing to do, it's a business imperative. We know that engaging all of our team members fully means that we can better serve a wider market, and we can increase involvement in our community service activities, such as our Youth of the Year program at Boys and Girls Clubs of America and our Driving My Financial Future program with Girl Scouts of the United States. Such programs don't just benefit the community, they benefit our team members, and they benefit our business.

Toyota Financial Services President and Chief Executive Officer, **Michael R. Groff**

From *The Corporate Citizen* magazine, Issue 12, 2015.

Other ways to encourage employee engagement are to increase investments in causes favored by employees, matching employee gifts when possible, and asking their opinions on potential programs. If you're totally focused on science, technology, engineering, math (STEM) education, for example, and your employees are privately giving to food pantries/banks and cancer support, you have ways to acknowledge their priorities without requiring a financial gift. Why not invite employees to contribute to the decision about what partner you choose, or increase the matching gift when their giving aligns with the company's cause? Recognition and participation incentives drive more impact by enhancing employee engagement and ultimately retention, strengthening local communities and your license to operate; well-publicized programs can even enhance your reputation and position in the marketplace.

As with all other elements of your corporate citizenship, your corporate giving program should be designed to advance one or more elements of your business strategy and to influence specific stakeholders.

TRENDS IN EMPLOYEE GIVING

More than 75% of companies report offering employee giving programs as part of their overall corporate giving programs.[1] The most effective programs are designed to offer employee choice and year-round giving options as well as payroll deduction and reporting. In addition, we see the following trends emerging among those companies that report the best outcomes from their programs.

PROVIDE ENGAGEMENT OPPORTUNITIES FOR VARYING EMPLOYEE SEGMENTS

Employees at different stages and levels are motivated to give and participate in corporate philanthropy and volunteer programs differently. Recognizing this, companies are offering more choice in their programs. Employees on a leadership track, for example, may be motivated to participate in a company's philanthropic strategy for the recognition, the exposure to executives, and the leadership opportunities. More junior employees may be more inclined to give time and to participate in employee-directed activities.

LEVERAGE TECHNOLOGY TO DRIVE ENGAGEMENT

The introduction of more choice certainly brings opportunity for companies and their employees to express shared corporate and personal values through workplace giving campaigns. Some of the innovations in campaigns that have been enabled by better technology have presented challenges to the traditional community affiliates. The level of engagement with federated giving organizations (such as local United Ways) varies significantly by geography. Federated campaigns (and organizations) are not being abandoned, but they are being challenged to change the way they solicit and operate.

Similar to volunteer programs, workplace giving can have a positive impact on employee attitudes toward their companies. According to a 2013 study, participation in giving programs can help employees identify with their organizations more as a whole, which in turn can improve commitment and loyalty.[2]

MOVING TO STRATEGIC GIVING

Although all of these approaches offer benefits, the greatest of these to your business, your cause partner, and your community comes from philanthropy that connects the purpose and commitments of your company with a relevant cause that delivers a measurable societal impact. This strategic approach is called many things in business journals such as "shared value," "collective impact," or "strategic philanthropy" to name just a few. Examples would be a beverage company supporting water organizations, confectioners helping develop human rights safeguards in the sugar or cocoa supply chain, or IT companies investing in programmer diversity and STEM education programs. In each case, the cause is related to an operating context issue that enables the company's success and requires a strategic partnership to unlock important benefits. These types of programs typically develop over years, and often from ideas that emerge from smaller partnerships.

The secrets to deriving the most benefit for all are:

- Make the connection between your cause and your company so obvious and logical that it would be evident to almost anyone who hears about it. When this is the case, stakeholders will assign more credibility to your company for commitment to the issue, as well as for having the expertise to make good investments.[3]

- Be upfront about the fact that your cause is important for society and your business. Research shows this also builds trust among your stakeholder groups, as they see your commitment as both strategic and an authentic commitment.

- Invest for the long term with strong and strategic partners. At the Boston College Center for Corporate Citizenship, we see the longer that companies invest in their signature causes, the more successful they are in achieving the business and social objectives of the giving commitment. Don't approach this as a marketing campaign. The longer you invest, the more likely your stakeholders are to remember your program, and the more they can see how committed you are to your cause. This can lead to many business benefits, including increased trust and more sales.

From the Corner Office

Managing Community Relations during Change

Being engaged in the community has been an important part of our history at Blue Cross Blue Shield of Massachusetts (BCBSMA), from our earliest days through current times.

Six years ago, we took a big step in becoming a more strategic player in the corporate citizenship space. We developed a focused approach that aligns with the company's mission of improving health, as well as the needs of the broader. We created four areas of emphasis: Healthy Child Development; Education Enrichment; Healthy Environments & Family Nutrition; and Sustainable Healthcare, with specific goals in mind for each category.

This past year, we reexamined our corporate citizenship strategy to ensure that we are the most effective corporate partner to our community, as well as a strategic partner to business areas within the company. Our approach was guided by three principles: be inspired by the community; be aligned with our corporate strategy; leverage sustainable financial investments and the leadership of our employees.

We conducted a landscape scan to measure our external efforts. The result for us is a new, sharper focus on Healthy Living.

An important part of our plan was the development of a comprehensive communications strategy to educate internal and external constituents. We met with executive leaders and employees at all levels across the company to establish support and develop champions for this strategy. Next, we capitalized on an annual community partner reception to connect with over 200 community partners about our platform.

With this input, we created specific goals within each of our three focus areas. We realize that there is going to be a reduction in the number of nonprofit partners that we work with. The nonprofit community is respectful of meaningful change and appreciative of transparency in the process. Therefore, as part of our rollout, we continue to meet with as many nonprofit and business leaders across the state as possible to socialize our new strategy. We've established clear guidelines for potential partnerships and created a specific review processes for all our activities to help us be a more effective corporate partner.

As we've gone through this transition, engaging internal and external stakeholders we've been able to communicate progress on goals and have asked for and received helpful feedback.

It doesn't get much better than that!

Blue Cross Blue Shield MA Vice President of Corporate Citizenship & Public Affairs, **Jeff Bellows**

DEVELOPING STRATEGIC PARTNERSHIPS WITH NONPROFITS

Once you have narrowed the focus of what you are going to do, you can begin to think about your larger initiatives. Say the issue you want to address is water. You'd like to develop a signature program related to water, and there are thousands of organizations that address water stewardship. The first step is to narrow the pool to those organizations that are working on the aspect of water (or arts or education) that is relevant to your program.

Nonprofits are differentiated in much the same way that companies are. Ask others working in the space who they respect, where the best thinking and implementation are happening. Spend time doing research. Send your staff to conferences on the issues you seek to affect. This is where it gets hard, but it's also where the strategic impact happens. Once you have a short list, work through the following questions to determine what your strategic giving program will look like.

1. *What's the focus of your giving?*
   To answer this, it's worth asking yourself some further questions:
   o What's the issue you're seeking to address? Environmental concerns, education, arts and culture, or something else? What change or outcome would you like to affect?

   o Where will your action be directed? At home or abroad? Globally, regionally, or within a country or community?

   o Who will it help? A specific age group, gender, or population such as rural or ethnic?

   o Why is addressing this issue important to your business?

   o How will you address it? How will you measure progress? How much should you give? Should it be based on need, available funds, time, networks, or experience? Will you act alone or as part of a network with other funders?

2. *What should your company give, and how should you give it?*

Cash is the obvious gift, but how about expertise, knowledge (intellectual capital), or products? Employees and suppliers can also contribute by giving time or money, or even business-related resources such as supplies, space, or infrastructure support.

3. *Why is your company uniquely positioned to support the mission of this nonprofit partner?*
Your organization needs to have a logical connection to your partner in order for it to be viewed as credible by your stakeholders. This strategic connection can come from a market opportunity, your operating context, your employee interests, or from a disaster or other event that affects people or places important to your business. Ask yourself:

o Does this partner share your company's focus, and a vision for how the issues to be solved can most efficiently be addressed?

o Are they a good brand and culture fit?

o Are you and the nonprofit aligned on the ultimate shared outcomes you seek to deliver?

Answering these three questions will help you to assess strategic fit. Once you have done this, your staff can conduct the operational due diligence to ensure that the partner is prepared and able to engage.

GIFTS DRIVEN BY RECIPROCITY

Some corporate gifts are driven by business relationships. Take the example of the rotating funding of gala dinner tables (I'll buy a table at yours if you buy a table at mine). If only a few people in the company interact with the cause, the result (as you may already have observed) is corporate names on empty tables. So instead of doing that, think first if you really need to attend a charity gala dinner (many nonprofits are actually moving away from them as the overhead is often high), or if you can donate the table or give in another way. If you feel you must buy a table, consider using the event as an employee leadership development opportunity. If it's for an educational institution, invite students. Be creative. In our work with various companies, we see the savviest executives filling gala tables with high-potential team members who are being evaluated for how they perform in that social environment as part of their job performance.

MANAGING AND MEASURING YOUR DIVERSE PORTFOLIO

It's much easier to measure the results of your corporate giving program if you're working with a small number of larger philanthropic commitments than a myriad of smaller ones. Why? Because it's more difficult to measure the effects of many small transactions than a couple of large ones.

When should you measure social impact? This can be tricky. If you're working toward specific social impact goals, you may need a nonprofit partner to help you measure the outcomes that indicate progress toward your goals. If measuring progress is important to you, you'll have to consider the potential cost of paying for assessment as part of the project. Smaller charities usually don't have the resources to provide detailed assessment data unless it's a budgeted part of your project with them.

THE VALUE OF EMPLOYEE VOLUNTEER PROGRAMS

With longer working hours and shorter tenures, it's more difficult than ever to keep employees engaged with their jobs. Engaged employees are people who are psychologically committed to their jobs, and likely to be making a positive contribution to their organizations.

In the Boston College Center for Corporate Citizenship's *Corporate Community Involvement Study 2015,*[4] more than 90% of companies identified increased employee engagement as one of the top three benefits of their volunteer programs. Sixty percent of companies with volunteer programs evaluate the relationship between employee volunteer programs and employee engagement. Among those that did, close to 90% of companies that measure the correlation between on-the-job volunteering and employee engagement found a positive correlation between employee participation in these programs and employee engagement scores. This demonstrates that employees who participate in corporate volunteering report higher commitment and loyalty to their company than their peers who do not. Many companies also believe that engagement, done right, should also drive business value vectors as innovation, productivity, and retention of high-performing employees. Some progressive employers are seeking to measure and manage this dynamic of engagement as well.

Employees May be More Motivated by the Opportunity to Do Well Than to Do Good

While the desire to do good in the community may be the reason many employees decide to volunteer *outside* of work, it's not what drives them to participate in corporate volunteer programs. Instead, many are drawn by skill development and networking opportunities. Think about how you can harness this for your program.

Companies that initiate employee recognition programs to acknowledge the community work undertaken by their employees report an average employee participation rate of 41%, compared to just 23% among companies that do not offer such programs.[5] What's more, employee volunteer programs, particularly for those that are strategic and engage employees through recognition, can help companies increase employee engagement and ultimately reduce the costs of turnover and low productivity.

Amplifying Employee Efforts as Part of Your Company's Commitment to the Community

Companies clearly recognize the value of employee volunteer programs in attracting prospective employees, as well as retaining their current workforce. Nearly 60% of companies include information about their volunteer programs during employee recruitment,[6] which is consistent with recent research that found prospective employees were more drawn to a company when their corporate citizenship efforts were illustrated in their corporate materials.

To communicate volunteer efforts effectively, you need to think about how to engage employees at different stages in their careers. While only 9% of companies consider the opportunity to identify future leaders as a top benefit of employee volunteer programs, research finds employees in the earlier stages of their careers (aged 18–39) are most motivated by career development and promotion opportunities. Older employees (aged 55–66 and above) however, are most deeply engaged by supervisor support and recognition.[7] Moreover, in the Corporation for National and Community Service's *2014 Volunteering and Civic Life in America*[8] report, people aged between 35 and 44 were most likely to volunteer, closely followed by those between 45 and 54.

You can also make use of employee volunteering in your company's team-building and development. Almost 80% of organizations offer volunteer programs to managers to help them develop their teams, and more than 20%[9] of companies that offer volunteer programs also incorporate volunteer participation feedback within their employee performance reviews. Ten percent even provide financial incentives for participation.

Business executives and corporate citizenship professionals clearly agree: community involvement contributes to reputational and employee-related business goals. In the Boston College Center for Corporate Citizenship's *State of Corporate Citizenship 2017*[10] survey, the majority of executives across all industries reported community involvement contributed to overall company success. The study also reveals it even contributes to business goals which aren't directly or obviously related to corporate giving or employee volunteering. For example, half of energy companies say that community involvement helps improve risk management, while more than half of food companies report that it contributes to securing a sustainable supply chain.

Organizing employees to volunteer and support these issues can be a great way to amplify the effects of your cash gifts, raise awareness for the cause your company is committed to, and develop skills and goodwill among your employees.

DOES YOUR COMPANY NEED TO ESTABLISH A CHARITABLE FOUNDATION?

Once you've thought through your corporate giving program strategy, you'll need to work out which vehicles you'll use to make your philanthropic commitments.

A lot of companies ask us if they need to set up a charitable foundation to implement their strategy. The short answer is probably not, unless you work for a highly regulated industry such as pharmaceuticals or medical devices (which have strict rules governing how much influence they can exert in related areas) or want to make grants to individuals (for instance, a scholarship program or prize). You might also want to consider a charitable foundation if you intend to create a permanent endowment to support your corporate giving, or plan to solicit gifts from others in support of your cause priorities. However, unless you fit one of these criteria, you can probably do everything you want to through a strategic corporate giving program, rather than establish a stand-alone, legally structured private foundation. Consult general counsel or a philanthropic advisor for insight on the best way to structure for your purposes.

10 QUESTIONS TO ASK YOUR TEAM BEFORE YOU MOVE ON

1. Have we defined the core focus and strategic intent of our corporate giving? Can we describe what we are trying to deliver succinctly — to our business and to our community?

2. Have we decided what the balance should be between strategic (company strategy related) giving and tactical (employee engagement) giving?

3. Can we describe the parts of our corporate giving strategy that support core strategic causes, employee engagement, community needs, and those informed by other drivers (such as legacy, reciprocal arrangements, and causes championed by executives)?

4. Do we or will we leverage a Corporate Foundation or Corporate Giving strategy or a combination of both?

5. Do we know which causes our company is already donating to or investing in, and why?

6. Do we have records of what's been donated in the past, and the measurement of results from these donations?

7. Have we identified a set of prospective new partners, based on the criteria provided in this chapter?

8. Do we have measurement plans and agreements in place?

9. Do we have reporting and communication mechanisms to leverage results with employees, communities, and external stakeholders?

10. What is the unique or differentiating aspect of our corporate giving strategy when compared with our sector, competition, or geographic peers?

NOTES

1. Boston College Center for Corporate Citizenship (2015).

2. Grant, Dutton, and Rosso (2008).

3. Becker-Olsen, Cudmore, and Hill (2006).

4. Corporate Community Involvement Study (2015).

5. *Ibid.*

6. Boone, McKechnie, and Swanberg (2011).

7. *Ibid.*

8. https://www.nationalservice.gov/newsroom/press-releases/2014/new-report-1-4-americans-volunteer-two-thirds-help-neighbors. Accessed on April 9, 2017.

9. Community Involvement Study 2015.

10. The State of Corporate Citizenship (2017).

SECTION 3

PULLING IT ALL TOGETHER

9

GETTING YOUR MESSAGE ACROSS

Communicating persuasively and effectively is absolutely pivotal to the success of your corporate citizenship program. Multiple research studies prove, time and again, that communication is a necessary ingredient to deliver maximum social and business value from your company's corporate citizenship investments.[1] Without increasing awareness to build support and report results, even your best plans will fail to deliver their full potential. Executives have a special role to play in communications. As a visible leader, many audiences look to you to set the tone and deliver messages to your broader audiences.

This means your messages in all channels and to all audiences need to be crystal clear: simple, limited, truthful, incorporating both values and facts. Ideally, they should include a call to action as well. Why a call to action? Because all corporate citizenship work is about driving *change*.

COMMUNICATING TO DRIVE CHANGE

To get people on board with your envisioned transformation, you must let them know what you want them to do — and even more importantly, what the opportunity is to make things better. Your work is not about preserving the status quo. You want to protect and build your company's reputation while you create more business and social value. By the very nature of that aspiration, you need to move people from where they are today to some new place: a more desirable future state for both your business and society.

The biggest mistake leaders make when they're trying to get people on their side is to assume what's important to them (the communicator) is also important to their audience. Not as a matter of judgment, but as a matter of fact, this is simply not true most of the time. So when you communicate with them, you want to identify and address the issues that are most important to *them*, keeping in mind that those things may be different from what is top-of-mind for you. In other words, it's not about what you *need* to say but about what they *are able* to hear and the actions they *want* to take.

Additionally, you need to communicate consistently and often. It can be hard to believe, but people need to read, see, or hear a message at least 3–5 times on average in order to recall it.[2] So when you can't stand to hear yourself say something once more, it's probably the first moment your audience really hears it. You need to keep repeating! Those busy lives we talked about earlier mean their attention is usually far from your cause; it takes a lot of repetition for even a simple statement to move from awareness to action.

This gap between your audience's daily experience and your own can lead to what we call "the curse of knowledge." You are an expert about your business and your industry. It's easy to forget your audience doesn't have that same knowledge. So think about using simple language and speak in their terms to fully explain the concepts. Speak in ways your grandmother could understand about the change you're trying to create. Questions your communication should answer for listeners might include:

- What? What's the key idea you're trying to communicate (in words a fourth grader could understand)?

- So what? Why is this issue important?

- What does it mean to me? How might this affect the person listening and how might is affect them?

- Now what? What do you want them to do?

HOW TO CREATE A COMPELLING CALL TO ACTION

There are several great books on the topics of influence and the key principles of the psychology of persuasive communications. Whether you refer to Robert B. Cialdini's *The Psychology of Influence*, Heath and Heath's *Made to Stick (one of Dave's particular favorites)*, Frank Luntz's *Words that Work*, or Malcolm Gladwell's *The Tipping Point*, you'll find they share common principles about what constitutes persuasive communication. You can put these to good use when you're managing your relationships with both internal and external audiences. Here's a construct we've developed that leverages elements of all four; it can help you to remember all the functional attributes you should be trying to build into your communications. A good message T-R-A-V-E-L-S.

Time-sensitive: the most effective communications have time boundaries. We find things more attractive when their availability is limited, or when we stand to lose an opportunity unless we act. The fear of losing out is a powerful motivation that drives people to mobilize in response to messages that employ this tactic; this is popularly called the "fear of missing out" (FOMO). For instance, we might buy something if we're told it's the last one or that the special offer will expire soon. If you can make your communications and appeals time-bound, you're likely to have greater success in getting people on board with your requests. Creating a deadline or limiting enrollment in a program could work well to activate this part of our human nature.

Rational: human beings have a deep desire to be consistent. Although we often respond to the emotional elements of appeals, our minds will work hard to justify why this would be a good decision. For this reason, once we've made a first, small commitment to something, we're more likely to take a larger next step which is consistent with it. This means giving your audience opportunities to rationalize their commitment is a good tactic. For instance, you'd be more inclined to support a colleague's project if you'd show an interest in it when he first talked to you, or to serve on a task force after you'd already been invited to review a document outlining the scope of the work.

Humans like to think they are rational and prefer to respond to facts (even when we are not doing so). So use specifics in your communications; these lend credibility to the rational evaluation of your message by your audience, especially when you want to prove larger assertions.

Context is important here, too. Focusing on the proportion of children who don't get breakfast at home (1 in 10) means more to people than simply giving the total number of children; the relationships between numbers are often more important than absolute values because they help to describe the context and magnitude of issues.

Action-oriented: remember that corporate citizenship is ultimately about driving change. Your intention is to continually improve your company's ESG performance and the world in which you live; these are huge goals which require influence far beyond the reach of your individual audience members. If your "ask" is too ambitious, they'll file the action under "maybe later, when I've retired"; instead, try to make it something they can do right now, today.

Validating: as humans we tend to be hyper-aware of what other people in our group are doing. When we were cavemen, we looked to the behavior of the herd to stay safe; now this is how we establish norms, which is basically another way of staying safe. Two tactics you can use to activate validation are safety in numbers and authority.

If your communication establishes that "everyone is doing it," you're more likely to persuade others to participate, especially if the "everyone" is a group your audience feels an affinity with or aspires to be in. You can establish affinity and identification in multiple ways. We often seek validation from people we like, and likability comes in many forms: people similar to or familiar to us, people who've given us compliments, or people who are magnetic or attractive. You can activate this principle by creating communications that acknowledge the values of the listeners and in a tone that's welcoming to the people you want to get on board.

You can activate the idea of authority in a number of ways as well. If you or your board is involved and it's clear your corporate citizenship program is important to you, others are more likely to get involved. Job titles, uniforms, and even gadgets can lend an air of authority that can validate your work. For you, your position, in-depth knowledge about the company and its community is a source of authority. Authority is also something that can be conferred; you can create and then reinforce the authority of others in your communications, by identifying them as expert resources for instance.

Emotional: although people want to be logical in their decisions, research tells us time and again that we're tremendously influenced by emotion. We tend to recall the way a communication made us feel more easily than its actual substance. This is because emotions are a form of disruption to our usual state. They move us out of equilibrium into a state of arousal that requires a different way of engaging with the world. This means more of our brain is involved with the communication we're experiencing, which in turn helps us to remember it. People are also more likely to spend more time with communications that surprise them or leave questions unanswered. In a now well-known study, researchers sent a letter requesting a group of psychologists take an action; half of them got the full letter which included a call to action in the conclusion, and the other half got only the first page which ended with a dangling clause. The recipients who only got the half letter responded to the experimenters in far greater numbers than those who got the full call to action. Their feelings of surprise and discomfort at not having the full picture motivated them to act. There's a well-documented psychological reason for this; if everything seems normal we don't pay much attention, but the minute we experience disruption to our understanding of the world we become alert.

You can also activate your audience's feelings toward others in order to increase the persuasiveness of your messages. We are social beings and tend to want to treat others as they treat us. This can lead us to feel that we must help other people if they have helped us. The key to success in employing this tactic is to be the first to give and also to personalize your giving to the recipient.

Humor can be an incredibly important emotion to get people to pay attention to your message. Think about the Ice Bucket Challenge; the power of this was in the delight we got from seeing CEOs and celebrities get into their skivvies and throw water over themselves. We love to see the humanity in people, and laughter is something we all share. So pulling on the heart strings is important, and humor is often what seals the deal.

How does this help your communications? By employing a range of emotions — from outrage to humor — and by including an element of unexpectedness, you can make them much more memorable.

Limited: this element is critical in the age of digital technology. Think 140 characters, 2.5 by 5 inches, and visual. The first is the number of characters allowed by Twitter, the second is the average screen real estate on a mobile screen, and the last is the attribute that will make your message much more likely to be opened. Communications are not something we sit down to receive; we process them 24/7. Recent research from the Pew Trust tells us that the average American receives more than 3000 messages across all channels in any given day. Combine this with the fact that 55% of people need to hear something between three and five times before they can recall it, and another 20% need to hear it as many as 10 times. These two points taken together underscore the importance of limiting your communications only to the most salient points. You should be able to capture your core message in 25 words or less, offering richer explorations to your audience as they become more engaged with your content.

Simple: recall and repetition go hand in hand. Try to write your message in a way so anyone can understand it. Your audience doesn't know everything you do, nor do they need to, so keep your communications at their level. Clear, uncluttered statements repeated over time will have a dramatic effect. You can simplify things by staying focused on what your message means for a specific audience member. If your communication is for a mass audience, think of the motivations that speak to each group. For example: "for our leadership this is a staff development tool, for our company this is a way to integrate with our community, for our employees this is a way to add interest to their jobs, and for our communities this is an essential health improvement initiative."

Remember: elementary language, short sentences, and vivid images work well.

CATHEDRAL THINKING

Cathedral thinking[3] is a term used to describe the act of envisioning, and then getting others to share and act upon a vision for the future. If you recall your history lessons, you'll remember that the Middle Ages was the golden era of cathedral building in Europe. As you can imagine, creating these amazing places of worship was not a simple matter. With the rise of the trades, skilled craftsmen were becoming mobile and able to demand to be paid in currency; this meant they were free to sell their services to the highest bidder. So community leaders needed to inspire these workers to commit to the project by creating vivid images of what the future was destined to be.

The community leaders' extra challenge was that because a cathedral took decades to build, some workers would never see the end results of their labors; they could only trust that by the time their grandchildren were born the work might be approaching completion. Those who

were sponsoring these massive edifices that took generations to build were building not only structures but also
real and symbolic monuments to ideals important to their
society. These were buildings that communicated big
ideas and served big purposes. So their communications
were not only aimed at the individual workers who
started the job, but also targeted toward the successive
generations who had to continue the building process.
They had to inspire them about the functional, social,
and emotional benefits involved. On a functional level,
they were paid to do the work; on a social level, they
were part of the craft community; and on an emotional
level, they were in service to the greater glory of their
God and the nobility who funded the projects. You can
see how, from the time of the inception of Western civili-
zation, we've activated these different motivations in people in order to get the best out of them.

So what are your cathedrals? They're the vivid images
of how things will be different if your corporate citizenship initiative works out as you intend. How can you
make your audience understand what that will mean to
them, to your communities and to their business enter-
prises, now and tomorrow? Do you know what success
looks like? How will your workplace, community, and
marketplace be different once you've achieved it: what
will it look and feel like to them? Can you describe it succinctly to each of your audiences in their language, in a
way that helps them see the benefits, and with visual
images that trigger an emotional response? What details
would bring it to life?

Being able to describe what success looks and feels like
is critical to achieving every aspect of strategy, whether

you're the CEO or an intern. Test it out in your own communications and challenge others to do the same.

Emotions come from the vision you paint for your audience. Have you helped them to imagine a world in which all children achieve to their best potential because they've eaten a healthy breakfast? What would it be like for every family to sit down to a nourishing, home-cooked meal at night because the parents have the time, resources, and skills to cook? Get people excited about the potential, about what can be achieved. Dig into your own emotions so that you can convey them to your audience.

10 QUESTIONS TO ASK YOUR TEAM BEFORE YOU MOVE ON

1. Have we done an audit of all our current corporate citizenship communications? Do we know what goes out when and to whom?

2. Do they live up to the standards we went through in this chapter?

3. If not, have we worked out how to address this going forward?

4. Have we discussed the tone and timing of internal and external communications as a team?

5. Have we identified our audiences and the actions we want each to take in response to our communications?

6. Have we thought about the WIIFM for each audience to whom we communicate?

7. What are the key functional, social, and emotional needs of each?

8. Do we understand the key elements of human nature that affect how we absorb communications?

9. Can we create some vivid and emotional stories that will help our audience feel more involved with what we do?

10. Can we describe what success looks and feels like in a business and a social context? What are our "cathedrals"?

NOTES

1. Margolis, Elfenbein, and Walsh (2007).

2. Edelman (2013).

3. Zakaria (2007).

10

BUILDING ON YOUR SUCCESS

Strategic corporate citizenship has the potential to transform your company at every level. Once you've made a commitment to implementing a comprehensive corporate citizenship program, the next step is to ensure those strategies systematically evolve and improve performance over time, which means developing management systems and reporting processes capable of integration and adaptation as your business evolves. This is important because if you do this correctly, your business can rely on the systems to improve and you can use your reporting not only to communicate the results you've achieved but also to manage future performance.

This chapter is about how to ensure the methods for executing your strategy include performance assessment and improvement plans, so you leave a system in place that helps your company excel for years to come.

USING EXTERNAL REPORTING AND DISCLOSURE TO YOUR ADVANTAGE

Reporting and disclosure are integral to your long-term success. Of course, reporting is nothing new; companies have been managing and disclosing performance metrics in one way or another for decades. What has changed recently is broader groups of stakeholders are now demanding increasing amounts of information about corporate performance far beyond financial boundaries. There are a number of reporting standards and guidelines that are global drivers for this; we won't cover them all, but we'll help you understand how the main ones work and their impact on you and your company.

Many of these reporting standards and guidelines organizations are working to harmonize with each other. With consistent external reporting, interested parties can see which companies are doing best in corporate citizenship within a sector, or even across sectors, and then decide where to invest their money or amplify the most authentic stories. The value of a reporting standard is it allows stakeholders to understand how organizations are performing on multiple dimensions in an "apples to apples" kind of way, providing a common language across international boundaries for understanding ESG performance. Standards and guidelines for reporting have evolved to the point where it's now an established industry.

The first and most widely known of these reporting frameworks was developed by a group known as the Coalition for Environmentally Responsible Economies (CERES). CERES created a global reporting framework in 1997 called the Global Reporting Initiative (GRI). This changed the landscape for corporate citizenship reporting forever, with the result that the GRI evolved into a stand-alone influential organization in its own right. The United Nations, for instance, has adopted the GRI reporting standard, and GRI has developed sector-specific reporting guidelines for areas such as utilities, financial services, oil and gas, and even food processing. Thousands of companies have adopted the GRI standard, and 95% of the 250 largest global companies use it. GRI's reporting framework has evolved to a reporting standard for ESG matters as of 2016[1] and just recently announced a transition toward becoming a set of topical standards. If you work for a large publicly traded company you may already be familiar with it, but even if not, it's important to understand a bit about what the G4 reporting framework consists of.

We could write an entire book just on this subject; in full disclosure, the Boston College Center for Corporate Citizenship is a certified training partner of GRI, the International Integrated Reporting Committee (IIRC),[2] and the Carbon Disclosure Project (CDP). All the major accounting firms around the world, and thousands of consultancies, have services to help companies compile these types of reports and assure some of the data. Building the capacity internally for this — even just to follow the GRI standard — is a significant investment, especially if your company is doing it for the first time.

GRI may be the most common globally adopted reporting standard but it's not the only one; there are different reporting structures for almost every sector, running into hundreds overall. Different than GRI, but related in many ways and broadly adopted, is the CDP. Started in 2000, it gradually evolved from a few voluntary questions for companies to answer about climate change policy and practice, to the comprehensive set of surveys it is today. More than 3000 companies now participate annually.[3] CDP also manages other extensive disclosure requests, and reports not just on climate change but also on supply chain, performance and operations, water disclosure, forest and fiber disclosure — there's even a report designed for cities.

Given that these reporting standards are voluntary, you may be wondering if you need to participate. CDP publicly ranks companies based on the information it receives. Major players such as Walmart, Dell, and PepsiCo use it as a way of ensuring sustainability within their supply chains; they actually send the report to their suppliers and insist it's filled out so that they can manage compliance through their sourcing procedures and practices. So CDP has gone from being a small assessment tool to being part of the corporate reporting infrastructure used by investors and companies themselves to manage environmental impacts throughout the value chain.

INTEGRATED REPORTING

This is a rapidly emerging trend, in which corporate citizenship reporting is increasingly being integrated into traditional financial reporting and ESG dimensions of business are evaluated using a perspective that incorporates financial, human, and natural capital — all as value-creating aspects of business.[4] For instance, in 2010 the U.S. Securities and Exchange Commission (SEC) added guidance for climate change risk reporting for all U.S. publicly traded companies.[5] Global stock exchanges, including those in the United States, have and will continue to integrate sustainability and corporate citizenship criteria into their listing requirements, which also has the effect of increasing standard reporting requirements. While we were working on this book, the U.S. SEC issued a request for public comments on the subject of integrating ESG topics into standard financial reporting guidelines. This landscape will continue to evolve.

Integrated reporting isn't only being driven by regulation, but also by companies who are experimenting with different ways of combining their financial and corporate citizenship disclosures. The benefit to corporations is they're able to show that they're trying to improve what they're doing, by being open about where it's working and where it's not. They are effectively saying that they would rather help create this and be a part of the journey than let it be dictated from the outside.

In the United States, one of the more interesting integrated reporting developments is being pursued by the Sustainability Accounting Standards Board (SASB). Their mission is to develop and disseminate sustainability accounting standards to provide decision-useful information to investors. SASB has issued sector-based disclosure standards.[6]

While integrated reporting may be slow to develop in the United States, the trend is clear. This is something for you to watch and learn from over the next decade.

LEVERAGING YOUR REPORTING

Investors, regulatory advisors, and to a certain extent your customers will increasingly be expecting companies like yours to participate in the large disclosure frameworks in the future. If you lead a publicly traded company almost anywhere in the world, you'll be included in certain investor indices and rankings whether you like it or not. More and more investment and research firms are analyzing your company, and investors are using these reports as a guide. The investment industry creates indices of the best companies in each sector or region; if you're a publicly traded company you're likely already ranked and profiled by more than one. Some of these lists are public, while others may be kept as research tools or sold to institutional investors as research intelligence.

Five to ten years ago, only socially responsible investors (SRIs) (SRIs are synonymous with ESG thematic investors — those investors or analysts that apply ESG screens to investment decisions) routinely reviewed corporate citizenship performance as part of their screening process. Today, ESG considerations are common, not only for SRI investors but also for large institutional investors such as pension funds and universities. These are hugely influential; it's estimated that they command more than 30% of the $100 trillion in capital invested globally.[7] With influential systems such as California's pension and retirement fund (CalPERS) making ESG performance criteria part of their investment screening process, others are likely to follow.

Some of these frameworks can be viewed as guidance alone to help you decide where to focus your efforts;

you'll want to make disclosures where you have the largest potential impacts and opportunities. By approaching reporting as a mode of communication that can drive change, you'll help your company make continuous improvements. It's very difficult for a company to go backward once they've committed; so reporting helps reinforce that advancement by providing a reminder of progress toward declared goals. Executives pay attention to those with financial influence and a stake in the company's long-term success.

As such, reporting processes are also an important opportunity to drive more accountability internally. Take the Dow Jones Sustainability Index (DJSI) for instance; this assessment tool, managed by RobecoSAM, covers just about every corporate citizenship angle you can imagine, from the supply chain and work force, to how you carry out training and development, to environmental, social, and human rights performance. It asks questions about what you do in manufacturing, how you implement eco-efficiency, and what your community affairs programming consists of. It even covers your stakeholder engagement and corporate giving and philanthropy.

As you can imagine, completing this assessment can be a significant investment of time and effort. However, survey time is also an opportunity for your internal team involved in the many dimensions of your company's corporate citizenship to directly engage in a number of topics and assess what they see coming down the pike. It also establishes a regular process for assessing all your firm's corporate citizenship commitments and ensure they are captured in a way that allows investors to decide which companies are managing their ESG impacts and opportunities most effectively.

You can also use your rankings and ratings to generate credible PR for your corporate citizenship strategy. Suppose your company has done a lot of work on improving employee engagement; if you pick the right platform and put some communication resources behind it, you could aim to receive recognition as a great place to work.

We suggest you view reporting as closing a loop in a continuous operation circle; strategies lead to programs and projects, measurable improvement and results, and more strategies and projects that build upon a cycle of continual progress. Each loop is a record of progress over time. Even if you're at the top of an index or external ranking, there will be places in your sector you are weaker than others. Finding opportunities for generating more value and combining them with what your stakeholders are thinking, your customers are demanding, and what you want to drive internally creates a potent force for change.

THE VALUE OF CORPORATE CITIZENSHIP

You know corporate citizenship isn't just about PR but also about developing a strategy and program that's integrated and permanent. It's not a six-month marketing program or an advertising campaign, it's a theme running throughout your company, anchored in your purpose, and leveraging your company's unique capabilities to deliver shareowner and stakeholder value. When your customers and consumers trust your values, they'll buy more readily from you. When your profits increase, you're able to invest in your business more purposefully.

This is the direction that most major corporations are going long term. It is not only the definition of success in the 21st century but also an enabler of that success. In order to keep up, your corporate citizenship strategy must be fully embedded within your business purpose and strategy. You need to build excellent and trusting relationships across the board, work with the key functions to drive enlistment, and communicate this with integrity and authenticity.

We've tried to provide you with the key tools to begin your journey. Now it's time for you to act. Remember, corporate citizenship always means asking other people to do their jobs differently and with a broader systems perspective and more ethical and external awareness. Your task isn't an easy one; changing things for the better never is. And the payback? You will deliver impact in society at the same time that you unlock the potential to increase your company's profits and the productivity of people in your organization.

That's 21 century corporate citizenship done well. That is how your company will win the battle for reputation and impact.

10 QUESTIONS TO ASK YOUR TEAM BEFORE YOU MOVE ON

1. Have we decided how we'll report and disclose our corporate citizenship performance?

2. Have we assigned accountability for corporate citizenship reporting and disclosure to an individual or team?

3. Do we understand the GRI and the reporting standards that might apply to our business?

4. Do we understand any legally required reporting and disclosure within our sector or regions of operation?

5. Do we understand the concept of integrated reporting?

6. Do we know about other major reporting and disclosure frameworks such as GRI, CDP, IIRC, DJSI, and SASB? And do we understand the different roles these organizations and others play in the reporting and disclosure landscape?

7. Have we identified other external assessments, including investor and analyst assessments, sustainability ranking methodologies, and "best places to work" frameworks, that already rank our company or that we could use to benchmark against?

8. Do we know what our key customers and investors expect when it comes to corporate citizenship reporting and disclosure?

9. Have we created a process to use our reporting and disclosure information within our company to drive continuous improvement?

10. How are we using external assessments of our performance, rankings and ratings, or investor evaluations, to drive continuous improvement?

NOTES

1. https://www.globalreporting.org/information/news-and-press-center/Pages/GRI-Standards-moving-forward-after-public-consultation.aspx. Accessed on April 9, 2017.

2. http://integratedreporting.org/why-the-need-for-change/. Accessed on April 9, 2017.

3. https://www.cdp.net/en/info/about-us. Accessed on April 9, 2017.

4. http://integratedreporting.org/wp-content/uploads/2013/03/IR-Background-Paper-Capitals.pdf. Accessed on April 9, 2017.

5. https://www.sec.gov/rules/interp/2010/33-9106.pdf. Accessed on April 9, 2017.

6. https://www.sasb.org/sectors-2/. Accessed on April 9, 2017.

7. http://www.gsi-alliance.org/wp-content/uploads/2015/02/GSIA_Review_download.pdf. Accessed on April 9, 2017.

LIST OF KEY TERMS

With a growing number of companies investing in socially and environmentally sustainable practices, corporate citizenship has grown and diversified exponentially over its relatively short history. An overwhelming number of new terms and acronyms have become part of the lexicon of doing good. The following glossary gives you a quick reference guide for some of the more commonly used terms and acronyms.

Let's start with what you may call your program. Here are some of the most commonly used terms:

- Corporate Citizenship

- Corporate Social Responsibility

- Corporate Responsibility

- Responsible Leadership

- Sustainability

- Social Investment

- Environmental, Social, and Governance

Try to resist the temptation to debate what your program should be called; the semantics are less important than the fact you have a program with clearly defined goals and objectives. Pick the terms that most connect to your company's culture and intention, and then move ahead. We all know what you mean.

You need to know what the terms in this glossary mean, but they're not the most important place to focus for effective programs. Don't get distracted by the plethora of standards, frameworks, initiatives, and organizations. At the heart of your great corporate citizenship program are the issues most material to your company's business strategy and purpose. One or more of the concepts and organizations described in the glossary may be helpful to your efforts. If they are, by all means avail yourself of their resources, but be selective.

CORPORATE CITIZENSHIP GLOSSARY

B Corp Benefit Corporation: A title granted to companies that have been certified to meet rigorous standards of social and environmental performance, and have bylaws that take into account their impact on the environment, community, and employees.

B Lab: A nonprofit organization that offers certification to businesses to become "benefit corporations" which meet higher standards of corporate purpose, accountability, and transparency.

BoP Base/Bottom of Pyramid: a term referring to the number of people at the base of the global economic pyramid (4 billion), whose incomes are below $3000 in local purchasing power.

CDP Carbon Disclosure Project: an international, not-for-profit organization offering a worldwide system for companies and cities to measure, disclose, manage, and share vital environmental information.

CFP Corporate Financial Performance: a term referring to a company's overall financial health and ability to generate revenue.

CGI Clinton Global Initiative: founded by former President Bill Clinton, this organization brings together global leaders to create and implement innovative solutions to the world's most pressing challenges.

CO2e Carbon Dioxide Equivalent: a measure used to compare the emissions from greenhouse gases based upon their global warming potential.

CSP Corporate Social Performance: often used as a synonym for corporate social responsibility (CSR). CSP refers to a company's interaction with the community on economic, environmental, and social issues.

CSR Corporate Social Responsibility: efforts by businesses to work with stakeholders to achieve improved economic, environmental, and social performance, sometimes known as the triple bottom line and also identified as corporate citizenship or sustainability.

CVC Corporate Volunteer Council: local networks for companies to share effective practices and address community needs through workplace volunteering, many of which are affiliated with local community-based agencies (HandsOn Network, Volunteer Centers, and United Way).

DJSI Dow Jones Sustainability Index: a family of indices managed by RobecoSam Indices and S&P Dow Jones that track the stock performance of companies according to economic, environmental, and social criteria, offering a measurement by which investors can judge the sustainability impact of their investment choices.

EHS Environmental, Health and Safety: a traditional name for departments in organizations responsible for implementing and managing environmental and occupational health and safety programs.

EICC Electronic Industry Citizenship Coalition: a partnership of the world's leading electronics companies working to improve efficiency and social, ethical, and environmental responsibility in the global supply chain.

EMS Environmental Management System: a framework that assists companies in establishing control over operations in order to lessen their environmental impacts and increase overall efficiency.

ESG Environmental, Social, and Governance: a general term used to describe the three primary areas of import for companies focused on making their operations sustainable. These three performance dimensions are often highlighted and evaluated by companies in their sustainability reports.

EVP Employee Volunteer Program: a type of program that aims to engage employees while helping the local community.

FASB Financial Accounting Standards Board: a private, not-for-profit organization that develops the financial accounting standards for the private sector in the United States.

FSC Forest Stewardship Council: an independent, non-profit membership organization that protects forests by setting standards for responsible forest management under which forests and companies are certified.

GAAP Generally Accepted Accounting Principles: a set of concepts developed by the Financial Accounting Standards Board that determine how organizations in the United States prepare, present, and report their financial statements.

GASB Governmental Accounting Standards Board: an independent organization that establishes and improves standards of accounting and financial reporting for US state and local governments.

GHG Greenhouse Gases: gases that trap heat in the atmosphere causing the greenhouse effect that supports life on earth, but that can have dangerous effects if their concentrations increase too much.

GHG Protocol Greenhouse Gas Protocol: an international accounting tool for businesses and governmental organizations to track, calculate, and manage their greenhouse gas emissions. The protocol almost always serves as the benchmark for other greenhouse gas standards developed throughout the world.

GIIN Global Impact Investing Network: a nonprofit organization that works to increase the scale and effectiveness of impact investments, which are investments made in companies, organizations, and funds with the purpose of creating positive social and environmental impact in addition to financial return.

GIIRS Global Impact Investing Ratings System: a ratings system that measures the social and environmental impact of companies and funds. GIIRS likens its assessment system to that of Morningstar investment rankings and Capital IQ financial analytics.

GISR Global Initiative for Sustainability Ratings: an initiative whose mission is to design a generally accepted ratings framework for assessing the sustainability performance of companies.

GRI Global Reporting Initiative: a nonprofit organization that works toward a sustainable global economy by providing sustainability reporting assistance, specifically their widely known Sustainability Reporting Framework.

GSA General Services Administration: a federal agency that provides and maintains buildings, acquires goods and services, and promotes administrative best practices and efficient operations for the US government.

HIP Human Impact and Profit: a measurement and management tool that quantifies the products, services, operations, and management practices of sustainability and citizenship and is used both by corporations and investors.

IIRC International Integrated Reporting Council: an international coalition of regulators, investors, companies, standard setters, accounting professionals, and NGOs that seeks to create the most commonly used framework for corporate reporting. Their "integrated report" method encourages companies to consider all aspects of an organization in reporting (strategy, governance, performance, and prospects) to increase their value creation over the short, medium, and long term.

ISO International Organization for Standardization: a Swiss-based organization that brings together representatives from around the world to agree on voluntary international standards for products, services, and good practice, seeking to make businesses more effective and efficient.

IRIS Impact Reporting and Investment Standards: established by the Global Impact Investing Network (see GIIN), these performance standards are used by impact investors to determine and evaluate the social, environmental, and financial success of impact investments and the impact investment industry at large.

IVA Intangible Value Assessment: a tool that assesses companies' financially material risks and opportunities arising from environmental, social, and governance factors.

KPI Key Performance Indicators: areas of measurement by which companies can track their performance in relation to their business objectives, often utilizing target goals or ranges as benchmarks for future evaluation.

L3C Low-profit Limited Liability Company: a company focusing principally on charitable or educational goals that may make a small profit, as long as making a profit is not the primary purpose of the organization. L3Cs are often considered hybrid organizations between nonprofit and profit entities.

LCA Life Cycle Assessment: a measurement of the potential environmental aspects and impacts of any organization, product, or service. This assessment evaluates every stage of development, allowing for a "cradle to grave" estimation of environmental effects.

MDGs Millennium Development Goals: eight objectives officially established by the United Nations in 2000, from the eradication of extreme poverty, to the advancement of environmental sustainability, to halting the spread of HIV/AIDs; all to be met by a target date of 2015.

NCA Natural Capital Accounting: a type of accounting that measures the indispensable resources and benefits essential for human survival and economic activity provided by the ecosystem. Natural capital is commonly divided into renewable resources (agricultural crops, vegetation, and wildlife) and nonrenewable resources (fossil fuels and mineral deposits).

NGO Non-Governmental Organization: a not-for-profit group, principally independent from government, which is organized on a local, national, or international level to address issues in support of the public good.

OECD Organization for Economic Cooperation and Development: a global organization of representatives from 34 member countries that meets to advance ideas and review progress in specific policy areas, such as economics, trade, science, employment, education, and financial markets.

PRI Principles for Responsible Investment: the six principles of responsible investing supported by institutional investors who believe that environmental, social, and corporate governance issues can affect the performance of investment portfolios.

SASB Sustainability Accounting Standards Board: a nonprofit organization engaged in the development and dissemination of industry-specific sustainability accounting standards in the United States.

SDGs Sustainable Development Goals: The successor initiative to the Millennium Development Goals (MDGs) of the United Nations. The SDGs, officially known as Transforming our world: the 2030 Agenda for Sustainable Development is a set of seventeen aspirational "Global Goals" with 169 targets between them intended to eliminate poverty and reverse climate change.

SRI Socially Responsible Investing: values-based asset portfolio management.

SROI Social Return on Investment: a method to quantify and monetize the social value created by an organization's programs, especially those in the nonprofit sector. This process was created by an American company, REDF, in the 1990s and is widely used today.

SSRN Social Science Research Network: an organization devoted to the worldwide distribution of social science research, comprised of a number of specialized networks in each of the social sciences.

TBL Triple Bottom Line: a term, created by Sustainability founder John Elkington in the 1990s, encapsulating three particular assessment areas by which businesses and investors should measure value: economic, social, and environmental.

UNGC United Nations Global Compact: a global initiative established in 2000 that provides a principle-based framework for businesses to adopt more sustainable and socially responsible policies in the areas of human rights, labor standards, anticorruption, and the environment.

UNPRI United Nations Principles of Responsible Investing: a United Nations supported initiative convening investors to put the six principles of responsible investing into practice through investment decision-making and ownership practices.

REFERENCES

Becker-Olsen, K. L., Cudmore, B. A., & Hill, R. P. (2006). The impact of perceived corporate social responsibility on consumer behavior. *Journal of Business Research*, *59*(1), 46–53.

Boone, J. B., McKechnie, S., & Swanberg, J. (2011). Predicting employee engagement in an age-diverse retail workforce. *Journal of Organizational Behavior*, *32*, 173–196.

Boston College Center for Corporate Citizenship. (2015). *Community involvement study 2015*. Boston, MA: Trustees of Boston College.

Delmas, M. A., Etzion, D., & Nairn-Birch, N. (2013). Triangulating environmental performance: What do corporate social responsibility ratings really capture? *The Academy of Management Perspectives*, *27*(3), 255–267.

Dimson, E., Karakaş, O., & Li, X. (2015). Active ownership. *Review of Financial Studies*, *28*(12), 3225–3268.

Edelman. (2013). *2013 Edelman Trust Barometer*. Chicago, IL: Edelman.

EPA Sustainability Concepts in Decision-Making: Tools and Approaches for the US Environmental Protection Agency. (2012), p. 26.

EU Directive 2014/95. Retrieved from http://eur-lex. europa.eu/legal-content/EN/TXT/?uri=CELEX% 3A32014L0095

Flammer, C. (2015). Does corporate social responsibility lead to superior financial performance? A regression discontinuity approach. *Management Science*, *61*(11), 2549–2568. doi:10.1287/mnsc.2014.2038

Galbraith, J., Downey, D., & Kates, A. (2001). *Designing dynamic organizations: A hands-on guide for leaders at all levels*. New York, NY: AMACOM Division of the American Management Association.

Gardberg, N., & Fombrun, C. (2006). Corporate citizenship: Creating intangible assets across institutional environments. *Academy of Management Review*, *31*(2), 329–346.

Grant, A. M., Dutton, J. E., & Rosso, B. D. (2008). Giving commitment: Employee support programs and the prosocial sensemaking process. *Academy of Management Journal*, *51*(5), 898–918.

Intel Corporation. (2004). *Everything matters: Global Citizenship Report 2003*. Intel, Santa Clara.

KPMG AG Wirtschaftsprüfungsgesellschaft. (2010). Intangible assets and goodwill in the context of business combinations: An industry study, Advisory, KPMG AG Wirtschaftsprüfungsgesellschaft, a subsidiary of KPMG Europe LLP and a member firm of the KPMG network.

Lawrence, R. G. (2004). Framing obesity the evolution of news discourse on a public health issue. *The Harvard International Journal of Press/Politics*, 9(3), 56–75.

Luo, X., Wang, H., Raithel, S., & Zheng, Q. (2015). Corporate social performance, analyst stock recommendations, and firm future returns. *Strategic Management Journal*, 36(1), 123–136.

Margolis, J. D., Elfenbein, H. A., & Walsh, J. P. (2007). Does it pay to be good? A meta-analysis and redirection of research on the relationship between corporate social and financial performance. Ann Arbor, 1001, 48109-1234.

Mitchell, R. K., Agle, B. R., & Wood, D. J. (1997). Toward a theory of stakeholder identication and salience: Defining the principle of what and what really counts. *Academy of Management Review*, 22(4), 853–886.

New York Times. (2016). Laurence D. Fink's 2016 Corporate Governance Letter. *New York Times*, February 2. Retrieved from http://www.nytimes.com/interactive/2016/02/02/business/dealbook/document-larry-finks-2016-corporate-governance-letter.html?_r=0

Orlitzky, M., Schmidt, F. L., & Rynes, S. L. (2003). Corporate social and financial performance: A meta-analysis. *Organization Studies*, 24(3), 403–441.

Raffaelli, R., & Glynn, M. A. (2014). Turnkey or tailored? Relational pluralism, institutional complexity, and the organizational adoption of more or less customized practices. *Academy of Management Journal*, 57(2), 541–562.

Raithel, S., Wilczynski, P., Schloderer, M. P., & Schwaiger, M. (2010). The value relevance of corporate reputation during the financial crisis. *Journal of Product and Brand Management, 19,* 389–400.

Research Magazine. (2003, May). *Most widely held stock throughout the socially responsible fund industry.* Retrieved from http://csrreportbuilder.intel.com/PDFfiles/archived_reports/Intel%202003%20CSR%20Report.pdf, 2003 Report, p. 38.

Simmons, C. J., & Becker-Olsen, K. L. (2006). Achieving marketing objectives through social sponsorships. *Journal of Marketing, 70*(4), 154–169.

The State of Corporate Citizenship. (2017). *Boston College Center for Corporate Citizenship.* Boston: Trustees of Boston College.

Thomas, M. L., Fraedrich, J. P., & Mullen, L. G. (2011). Successful cause-related marketing partnering as a means to aligning corporate and philanthropic goals: An empirical study. *Academy of Marketing Studies Journal, 15*(2), 389–401.

Vitaliano, D. F. (2010). Corporate social responsibility and labor turnover. *Corporate Governance, 10*(5), 563–573.

Zakaria, F. (2007). Cathedral Thinking, concept first introduced by former Duke Energy Chairman and CEO James E. Rogers in 'Cathedral Thinking:' Energy's Future. Newsweek, August 20/27.

INDEX